Praise for
Jesus, Love, & Tacos

"Once again, my friend Carrie Stephens has mixed her witty writing with deep insights on the church and the power of community. She serves up this fun read at a time when all of us could use a plate of tacos and truth that leave the heart fed and challenged!"

—**Lynette Lewis,** TEDx speaker, business consultant, and author of *Climbing the Ladder in Stilettos*

"*Jesus, Love, & Tacos* is a vacation read, Bible study, and encouragement to the soul all wrapped into one delicious book of goodness. I loved every moment of reading the main text and could not wait to get to each new footnote. I laughed and held back tears as Carrie, with spirit-filled hope, took some of the hardest topics facing the Church today and graciously showed us how *Jesus, Love, & Tacos* can fix it!"

—**Rosalynn M. Smith,** PhD, Pastor of Mission & Adult Education at Mosaic Church Austin, and author of *A Prayer for Baby: A 40-Week Pregnancy Daily Devotional*

"Like queso oozing off your nachos, joy and encouragement drip from the pages of this book. I smiled the whole way through it. Carrie Stephens reminds us all that what we really crave comes from Jesus alone. Her authentic words will minister to your heart while tickling your tastebuds."

—**Heather Creekmore,** author of *Compared to Who?* and *The Burden of Better*, podcast host, and amateur Mexican food critic

"In *Jesus, Love, & Tacos*, Carrie Stephens invites us to a deeper understanding of ourselves and God. Through her vulnerable stories about her life and insights about communing with Jesus, Carrie shows us all what a spirit-filled life can be."

—**Shane Blackshear,** author of *Go and Do: Nine Axioms on Peacemaking & Transformation from the Life of John Perkins*

"Reading *Jesus, Love, & Tacos* is a bit like eating a mind-blowing taco: It's so delightful you devour it as fast as you can, laughing aloud between mouthfuls . . . but when you pause between bites, you realize it has quite a kick. The heat keeps working on you—in the best possible way. If you need an encouraging call back to Jesus, this book is for you. If you've been tempted to give up on church, this book is for you. If you've longed to reclaim the dream of godly community, this book is for you. *Jesus, Love, & Tacos* is a feast for the heart—the best kind of soul food."

—**Elizabeth Laing Thompson,** inspirational speaker and author of *All the Feels*, *All the Feels for Teens*, and the When God Says series

"With so many laugh out loud, 'yes girl, that'll preach,' and 'where's the lie?' moments, Carrie's wit and humor makes this book entertaining and so fun to read. It's like chatting with your cool friend at your favorite coffee shop while getting all the tea on how to live and love like Jesus. Carrie shares compelling biblical gems within the pages of this book . . . and if you could use a bit of comic relief like me, the footnotes are life."

—**Natasha N. Smith,** author, speaker, and host of *Can You Just Sit with Me?* podcast

"Soft or hard? The debate over which kind of shell to enjoy my beloved taco in is real! Similarly, disunity within the Church also exists, leaving us unsure of when the shells of our heart should be soft or hard toward sin and one another. *Jesus, Love, & Tacos* is a spicy mix of biblically based wisdom and wit that helps us answer this by curing our craving to deconstruct or distance ourselves from Jesus and his Church whenever they disappoint or hurt us. By feasting on Carrie's insights, you'll gladly accept Jesus's invitation to truly love his presence, his people, and yes . . . even tacos, regardless of their shell type."

—**Tracy Steel,** speaker and author of *A Redesigned Life: Uncovering God's Purpose When Life Doesn't Go As Planned*

A Spicy Take on Lordship, Community, & Mission

Jesus Love & Tacos

Carrie Stephens

TACOS FOREVER !

Carrie Stephens

LEAFWOOD
PUBLISHERS
an imprint of Abilene Christian University Press

JESUS, LOVE, & TACOS
A Spicy Take on Lordship, Community, and Mission

an imprint of Abilene Christian University Press

Copyright © 2022 by Carrie Stephens

ISBN 978-1-68426-082-9 | LCCN 2022014589

Printed in the United States of America

Published in association with Books & Such Literary Management, 52 Mission Circle, Suite 122, PMB 170, Santa Rosa, CA 95409-5370, www.booksandsuch.com.

LIBRARY OF CONGRESS CATALOGING-IN-PUBLICATION DATA
Names: Stephens, Carrie, author.
Title: Jesus, love, & tacos : a spicy take on lordship, community, and mission / by Carrie Stephens.
Other titles: Jesus, love, and tacos
Description: Abilene, Texas : Leafwood Publishers, [2022]
Identifiers: LCCN 2022014589 (print) | LCCN 2022014590 (ebook) | ISBN 9781684260829 |
    ISBN 9781684268962 (kindle edition)
Subjects: LCSH: Christian life. | Jesus Christ—Lordship.
Classification: LCC BV4501.3 .S7444 2022 (print) | LCC BV4501.3 (ebook) |
    DDC 248—dc23/eng/20220408
LC record available at https://lccn.loc.gov/2022014589
LC ebook record available at https://lccn.loc.gov/2022014590

Cover design by Greg Jackson, ThinkPen Design | Interior text design by Sandy Armstrong, Strong Design

Leafwood Publishers is an imprint of Abilene Christian University Press
ACU Box 29138 | Abilene, Texas 79699

1-877-816-4455 | www.leafwoodpublishers.com

22 23 24 25 26 27 28 / 7 6 5 4 3 2 1

For Morgan, Mosaic Church, and our great God.

I love dancing with all of you.

"Here are some good and greasy tacos from Wally's.
This is the closest you may ever get to tangible love.
I can't promise you'll enjoy the dinner I cook
tomorrow, so savor every bite of this one today."

—Me, to my family on the regular

CONTENTS

Here's the Taco Deal

"Life moves pretty fast. If you don't stop and look around once in a while, you could miss it."

—Ferris Bueller, *Ferris Bueller's Day Off*[1]

uenos dias, dear reader, *y bienvenidos* to a book about three of my most favorite things: Jesus, love, and tacos.

I assume we have a few things in common since you picked up this book. Forgive my presumptiveness, but I imagine you as the kind of person who takes your faith and your fajitas seriously. Maybe, like my friend Lisa, you have taken Communion before with tortilla chips because gluten-free Jesus is the best kind of Jesus for your gut to digest. Or perhaps, like me, you have gazed upon a plate of *tacos al carbon* after a three-day fast and found yourself in an I-was-born-for-such-a-time-as-this kind of Esther moment. Or maybe you just thought the cover of this book looked

---

[1] *Ferris Bueller's Day Off*, directed by John Hughes (1986; Los Angeles: Paramount Pictures).

interesting, and now you realize I'm the kind of person who might speak in holy, hushed tones about the best taco trucks in town as if they were the famed cathedrals of Europe.[2]

Despite my enthusiasm for all things taco-related, Jesus Christ is, of course, honored in this book above some guy named Sam who makes a mean Mr. Orange fish taco at Torchy's here in Austin.[3] But I hope you find Sam and all the rest of us here in these pages as well.

Jesus once assured his followers that they would have a lot of trouble in this world. I wonder what the trouble in your life looks like today as you read these pages. As I write this, the world is in almost 100 percent trouble; every nation in the world has been navigating the unpredictable and constantly changing world of a pandemic. I keep imagining you out there somewhere dealing with all the same confusing nonsense. We're having the best time in the 2020s, aren't we? Life these days is like a taco Tuesday party minus the tacos, music, or any fun whatsoever. Everyone seems fragile and weary about life in general. If the whole world could figure out how to live the gospel in community while handing out tacos, we just might make it through—which is precisely what this book is all about.

Personally, the quality of my life was on a serious uptick at the end of 2019. I was happily preparing for the release of my very first book, *Holy Guacamole*. I had speaking engagements slotted at conferences and churches. Our family had an unusual number

---

[2] The crazy thing is the best taco trucks are usually in gas station parking lots. They're also the riskiest places to eat in town because if they poison you, they can disappear and never be found again. May the Lord be ever leading you wisely, my people.

[3] If you're in Austin and have a hankering for fish tacos, a Mr. Orange will do in a pinch. But if you want my favorite fish taco here, go to Cabo Bob's. Or you could make a holy taco pilgrimage to San Diego and go on a fish taco expedition. You'll miss a few days of work, but it will be so worth it to sit by the Pacific and eat the blessed fruit of its depths.

of vacations planned to North Carolina, California, and (gasp) Italy in 2020. Our city, Austin, was thriving and growing, as was our church. We felt grateful and awed by the number and quality of people God had added to our community. Our to-do lists grew daily, but all the work felt positive and purposeful.

In December, we held 2020 in our hands like a precious stone ready to be placed in the perfect setting.

But then I went to a routine doctor's appointment to have routine tests done. The results were not routine, unfortunately. The doctors brought me back for more tests once, and then again. In the days of waiting for those test results, I practiced overthinking like I had made the team for the bad mental health Olympics. I forgot everything God had ever done in the history of the universe except the first three chapters of Job. If sickness and loss could descend on my new best friend Job and blot out his bright and happy life, then I was surely doomed.

Suddenly, 2020 seemed incredibly hazy. One phone call would determine my fate, and I chatted with God one day about the injustice of the potentially bad news. In case God had lost his omniscience, I reminded him about my plans. I pointed out that he had explicitly told me to write a book seven years before, and a healthy body was required to travel, speak, and adequately promote that book. I held up all the ministry happening in and through our church and suggested that unexpected and out-of-the-blue chemotherapy might interfere with God's original plans for 2020.[4] And then I took my selfish, heretical overthinking to a whole new level and told God I couldn't be sick because my husband and I needed to go to Italy to celebrate our twentieth wedding anniversary.

---

[4] I find that mixing bad theology with overthinking really wows the judges at the bad mental health Olympics.

At this point, the Holy Spirit decided I had pitched a big enough fit and airdropped the twenty-five years of biblical study I had trashed while overthinking back into my brain. I remembered how big God is and how small I am. I remembered how God is trustworthy and good. I saw my cries of injustice for what they were: fear. I was afraid of loss. I was afraid of sickness. I was scared of losing my connections with our church and all the people I care about. Once I admitted my fears to God, he spoke one very clear sentence into my heart: *Let me do something for you.*

While I'm sure there are plenty of people who would be encouraged by God's offer to do something for them, I was not. Those words made me uncomfortable. Think for a moment about all the people and situations in the Bible that required God's supernatural intervention. Think of Joseph left in a pit to die. Think of Moses getting yelled at by the Israelites about wanting meat to eat in the desert. Think of Mary and Martha watching over their sick brother, Lazarus, as he died. Think of the woman who snuck healing out of Jesus by grabbing onto his robes. Think of Peter sinking into the water after Jesus invited him on a wave-top stroll.

These miracles and God's interventions are all theoretically inspiring to read about, but I would rather be safely tucked in a comfy life than require them as uplifting testimonies.

In the middle of worship the following Sunday morning, I admitted to God that I would prefer not to need him to do anything for me. I'd like to be healthy, A-okay, and shipshape on my own. (You may be concerned that I am too honest with God. Perhaps I am; but in my experience, he is aware of my spicy attitude long before I realize it exists.) God rolled his eyes at me and pointed to the cross as an example of how far he is willing to go to do things for people, as well as evidence that we typically need his help far more than we realize.

My unsettling test results were not a new revelatory sign that I needed God to do something for me. His help and rescue have been indisputable and indispensable since sin entered the world. The whole message of the gospel is that God does for us what we can never do for ourselves.

I raised my hands in surrender to God and plopped my heart down in Jesus as I anticipated hearing the worst possible news from the doctors. No matter what report I received, God would do something for me.

When the doctor finally called with the results in January 2020, I nearly fell over when the voice on the other end of the line said, "The biopsy was negative. You have nothing to worry about." I hung up and immediately, instantaneously, thought two things. First, I didn't understand how this woman could imply that I had "nothing" to worry about. Worrying is like breathing; it keeps me alive! Overthinking and worrying are my favorite noncontact sports. Second, I was pretty sure God had been a little too dramatic with his offer to "do" something since there was apparently nothing to be done whatsoever. Couldn't he have just told me I was perfectly healthy because the test results would be negative?[5]

I considered that call an invitation to push the whole episode out of the way and press on into 2020. Indeed, we were beginning our most incredible year yet! Alexa, cue the book release party and lessons in Italian! Like the Jeffersons from *The Jeffersons* television show, we were movin' on up to the top! We had found our piece of the pie, and we couldn't wait to warm it up and scoop some ice cream on it.[6]

In our unfortunate tale of Carrie's lack of foresight, let's fast-forward to late March 2020. We did not move on up, nor was there any pie involved in 2020 except the humble kind. Instead

---

[5] God is kind of too much sometimes, isn't he?
[6] Personal note: make pie and ice cream part of my next book title.

of indulging in 2020 à la mode, I found myself canceling speaking engagements, plane tickets, and Airbnbs. Bookstores closed, leaving me with nothing to promote. My kids logged in to Zoom classes at home every day. Our church couldn't meet in person, and I missed our community deeply. Everything about life as we knew it changed because we were afraid of being sick.

In the shower one afternoon, as I washed my hair, I had a revelatory moment as I attempted to process some of my fear and sadness: the whole world was experiencing every loss a cancer diagnosis could cause. The pandemic transformed us all into Jobs. Shampoo ran down my face and burned my eyes, but I barely noticed. All I could see that day was how our way of life and plans had been wiped away.

Let me do something for you, God said again.

I realized then that I was the woman who heard the Word of God and missed the point entirely. When Jesus spoke about dying and being resurrected to his disciples, they remained naive about God's plans even as they listened to his words. I was the apple that hadn't fallen far from the tree of her spiritual ancestors. As I prayed about medical tests at the end of 2019, God was spilling the cosmic beans about a historic event poised in our future. I misunderstood his meaning and applied his promise to only my one small life. (That's the first time I have ever been overly self-involved regarding God and my prayer life. *Promise.*) I realized in the shower that day that God wasn't offering to do something for me about a biopsy; he was offering to do something for the whole world during a viral pandemic.

The "something" God wants to do begins with Jesus, God's great love for us, and our ability to fulfill his call to mission in the world. I would like to think that the "something" involves rescuing us from all the ways we have been horrible to one another as we fumble our way through this confusing time. However, I suspect God is allowing this storm of our circumstances to slosh us out of our fear and pain and into heightened awareness so he can wake us up (more on that much later in the book).

As random as this may be, this talk about God doing something kind of reminds me of the time I gave a designer sofa to God. I promise this isn't as much of a non sequitur as it may first appear.

My Sofa Named Samuel

To imagine God wanted or needed my designer sofa is ludicrous at best. The recipient of my sofa probably didn't necessarily want or need it, honestly. She thanked me and said she liked the new-to-her sofa, of course, but her life was not changed forever by a fancy hand-me-down sofa. My life, however, certainly was changed by the giving away of it, and this is the story of that.

For starters, you should know I retroactively named that sofa Samuel after the prophet in the Bible. Do you know the story from 1 Samuel 1 about Hannah and her longing for a child? Hannah was adored by her husband Elkanah but tortured because Peninnah, Elkanah's other wife, had borne children, while Hannah had not.[7] Hannah's life was like ours—a mixed bag of triumphs and trials. Hers was a pretty juicy tale, and I hope you enjoy my brief retelling of it.

Every year, when Hannah and her family went to Shiloh to worship and offer their sacrifice, Peninnah would taunt Hannah with her barrenness. One year, Hannah couldn't take it any longer (good for her). She went to the sanctuary and made a spectacle of herself as she asked God for a child. She promised to give the child to the Lord if he gave her one.

---

[7] If nothing else, let this story remind us that polygamy is garbage.

Hannah's behavior scandalized Eli, the priest of Israel, who accused her of showing up to church drunk.[8] But Hannah explained she was just a brokenhearted woman pouring her heart out to God. The priest then assured her that God would give her what she asked for, and Hannah believed this man, despite his unjust accusations of her.

When I consider this story in light of our modern ideas about church and community, I am awed by Hannah's singular lack of indignation toward both Peninnah and Eli. Hannah was a woman wounded by not one, not two, but three different enemies, all members of her "church." First, she was wounded by her community's insistence that physical barrenness equaled failure for any woman (proving we're not the first culture to struggle with mommy wars). Second, Hannah was wounded by Peninnah when she targeted her to degrade and discourage her. Hannah had to live alongside and worship with Peninnah despite their dysfunctional and painful relationship. Third, Hannah was wounded by Eli, who was, in a way, the lead pastor of the church she attended. Later in the book of 1 Samuel, we learn that Eli's sons were abusing the people who came to worship. Talk about a church scandal! This priest accusing Hannah of moral failure was on the struggle bus himself.

But Hannah didn't allow her pain to discredit God, her faith, her commitment to her community, or her willingness to offer her very best to God's mission in the world.

Do we live as courageously and faithfully as Hannah? How can we be this brave? Are we generous and gracious when we've been overlooked or unjustly accused? Or do we use the weaknesses of others to deconstruct our faith and/or our communities without offering to help birth a better future?

---

[8] This kind of makes one wonder: Just how many drunk people were showing up for Eli's services? Like, this was his go-to reaction?

When incredible, faithful Hannah gave birth to Samuel nine-ish months later, she didn't forget her promise to God. Once Samuel was weaned, Hannah took him back to that tabernacle so he could grow up there and serve the Lord with his life. And Samuel? Samuel went on to be God's chosen replacement as the priest after Eli and his sons collapsed under the weight of their sin. Samuel anointed Saul and then David as the first two kings of Israel. He faithfully served God and Israel to the end of his days. In large part, he had his mother to thank.[9]

Perhaps I'm biased, but I'm pretty sure Hannah was one of the most remarkable women to ever grace the earth. What would have become of Israel if she had lashed out at Peninnah instead of trusting God with her pain? Or if she had ignored her heart's cry and agreed with her husband, saying, "Yes, dear, my longing for a child is silly. I have you. What more can a woman want?" Or if she had abandoned her promise and kept Samuel for herself after she weaned him? I hope you'll tuck Hannah's story away as you read the rest of this book, because Hannah is a shining example of a person who can show us the way to God through our commitment to faith, community, and God's call. Amen, and amen.

Now, back to the "other Samuel," aka my designer sofa. How was my sofa a smidge like Hannah's son? (Cue epic movie trailer music and narrator's voice.)

When my husband and I bought Samuel the sofa, it was an unloved floor-sample sofa in an expensive boutique in downtown Austin.[10] We were dirt-poor campus ministers back then, and our budget for furniture was about zero dollars and five cents. I poured out my heart to my husband, Morgan, suggesting we

---

[9] Don't we all, though? #momsrock

[10] Remember when we used to leave our houses to go to actual stores to buy things? We didn't even necessarily know what they had in the stores because we couldn't look up what the stores sold online. It was fun and terribly inconvenient in the best way.

spend two months' rent on that down-filled, kiln-dried, wood-frame, chocolate-brown velvet sofa. I probably looked a little drunk on the dream of buying something we could not afford with money that could have furnished our whole apartment had we been standing in IKEA. My speech in favor of buying Samuel involved the following arguments: That sofa would last forever because I would vacuum, fluff, and flip the cushions weekly. We would not allow food on Samuel the sofa. We would raise our future children to love Samuel the sofa like a part of the family. If Morgan agreed to the sofa, I would be buried in a sofa-shaped coffin someday, wrapped in the loving memories of our family cozied up on Samuel for family movie nights, Super Bowl parties, and epic the-floor-is-lava game marathons.

My husband's irrational love for me mirrors Elkanah's love, and he agreed to buy the sofa. All was right in our sofa world for a few brief years. Then one Sunday, as we listened to a pastor speak about generosity, God reached out through the sermon and put his finger on our Samuel the sofa. Unlike Hannah, who knew that everyone and everything belonged to God first, I was shocked to realize God could claim our sofa as his own. The pastor mentioned that people tend to be more generous with their rattier belongings. He described the broken-down tennis shoes, uncomfortable chairs, and ripped towels we typically drop off at Goodwill. Then he suggested perhaps we could do better.

For context, I'd like to mention that the pastor who preached this sermon lived in a mansion on the golf course, and his wife once hung a twenty-thousand-dollar chandelier in her dining room. I suppose generosity was a stellar topic to preach about. Still, it would have been easy to be offended that he reached his hands into our mostly empty bank account instead of upending his own. Given the disparity of our bank account balances, we could have required him to make the first sacrificial move, just as Hannah could have insisted Eli go first and get his life in order before she brought Samuel to him. But during that sermon, God told me to give away our sofa. I was too surprised by the command to look for a way out.

I dreaded telling Morgan, though. I worried he would argue and remind me of my vows to care for Samuel the sofa like a child born of my own body. I wondered how humiliating it would be to insist we set that sofa out by the curb and let someone take it home. Would my husband ever trust me again when I insisted I knew the right thing to do?

Thankfully, I didn't have to find out the answers to any of those questions because, after church, Morgan looked at me and said—I kid you not—"Remember that part of the sermon about donating stuff? I think we're supposed to give away the sofa."

God has a way of working things out.

For a few weeks after Samuel left the building,[11] I wondered if I had accidentally sent with him a dominant limb necessary for breathing. The powerful sight of our empty living room highlighted how easily God can dissolve my logic, reason, and best-laid plans. Giving away our favorite sofa was proof that God cares more about the condition of our hearts than about the style of our living room. There were days I resented this truth as I sat on the ugly blue sofa that took Samuel's place. Replacing a resplendent sofa with an awful, floppy thing is a very "I am so privileged I even nauseate myself" kind of loss.

But looking back, I know this: in a small way, giving away my sofa was an attempt to enter into a Hannah-like space. While offering a sofa to God is a far cry from offering a child to God, almost twenty years after Samuel the sofa came into our lives, I see how

---

[11] He was not with Elvis, though.

God used that sofa to humble our hearts, increase our faith, and draw us into God's love for the people in our lives.

Like Hannah, we may have been accused of failure by the expectations of the cultural values upheld by our community. Like Hannah, we may have been targeted by people in the church who ought to have loved us better. Like Hannah, we may have been written off by church leaders as unfit in some way, only to later learn those leaders bore their own undealt-with weaknesses and sins. I know I have.

Samuel the sofa was just a thing made of wood, feathers, and velvet. What I needed more than a comfortable place to rest my backside was the lesson that opening my hands to God soothes the pain of my wounds when God's people and systems suggest I am insignificant in the larger story.

Hannah learned this long before I ever did. In 1 Samuel 2, she prayed a gorgeous prayer (later echoed by another great mother, Mary, in Luke's Gospel) after bringing Samuel to live in the tabernacle. In that prayer, she declared how great and mighty God is, highlighting how he fills his people despite the emptiness of their lives. My favorite part is verse 5: "Those who are full hire themselves out for food, but those who are starving hunger no more. The woman who is childless gives birth to seven, but the woman with many sons pines away" (1 Sam. 2:5 CSB).

I once faced an empty living room, but that's nothing compared to what's happened in the world lately. We have faced empty churches, schools, and grocery shelves more recently. Perhaps (likely) many years from now, the world will be emptied upside down in some other way.

But no matter the emptiness we face today, God wants to do something for us. We will explore that "something" in these pages through three concepts/metaphors. First, God wants to establish himself in our lives as our powerful, trustworthy authority in this time of uncertainty and change. We will begin with three chapters about Jesus, exploring how the lordship of Christ is a necessary, central piece of our faith as Christians. Second, God wants none of us to be left alone. Thus, we will move to three chapters about love as the foundation of community. My hope is that we can learn better how to "carry one another's burdens," as Galatians 6:2 teaches us, so that we might "fulfill the law of Christ." Last, God wants to open our lives and lift our hands so we can feed his hungry world. As we talk about tacos (it's honestly hard for me not to talk about tacos most days), we will be exploring how to join God in his mission in the world.

Welcome again to *Jesus, Love, & Tacos*. I hope to make Hannah, you, and all the other faithful women and men of God proud on these pages. But most of all, I pray God does something for each of us as we place our trust in his goodness.

Now, let's see what pupusas, Jesus, and El Salvador have to do with our faith. Because that's where we're headed first. Cue the dance music.

Part One

Jesus
_____

Responding to
His Lordship

Aligning Our Lives with Lordship

CHAPTER

1

Jesus
as the Boss of Us

"I'm on a mission. There's not enough love to go around.
My job is to find out why."

—The Boss Baby, *The Boss Baby*[1]

Once upon a time, twenty-five-ish years ago, a very White girl from Orange County, California, decided to major in Spanish at UCLA. I was that girl, and the time that was once upon us was 1996.[2]

I didn't technically speak much Spanish at the time. That significant life decision was motivated by credits for graduation and the quickest path to a diploma. Please feel free to have your high school seniors call me for college counseling advice. I am clearly a natural.

As it turned out, I was one of only a few nonnative Spanish speakers in most of my classes. Many of my classmates were first-generation US citizens whose parents had immigrated from

---

[1] *The Boss Baby*, directed by Tom McGrath (2017; Beverly Hills, CA: 20th Century Fox).
[2] Ah, the midnineties, when the Internet was mostly useless and we could all still read paper maps.

Spanish-speaking countries. These students were legitimately bilingual, whereas I faked my bilingualism hardcore. I trudged along most days, hoping my C average would score me a degree to get out of school and get on with *mi vida loca*. I kept my head down in class, clinging to the rules and vocabulary of the Spanish language like a lifesaving device.

Meanwhile, all around me, my friends chatted each other up in that beautiful language their mothers used to call them to breakfast. Spanish was the language they used to argue with their siblings about chores and to sing along with Selena on the way to the beach. Spanish was in my head, but it was in my friends' souls.

Thankfully, my classmates felt sorry for me, the *gringa* with good intentions. They tried to help shove Spanish into my soul. I was delighted that their method of soul ministry toward me involved massive quantities of food.

The soul of a culture is best encountered in the food of that culture, so my friends often took me to their favorite authentic restaurants. I ate one of the best meals of my life in a little Salvadoran restaurant on a backstreet in Los Angeles, where my *salvadoreña* friend introduced me to pupusas. Pupusas are delicious flatbreads stuffed with things like meat, cheese, and beans. They're the national dish of El Salvador, and if I ever start my own country, I may make them my national dish, too.

If you've never had pupusas, you have been the victim of a tremendous cultural tragedy. But quality pupusas aren't always easy to find. Without a trusted guide, I never would have found the restaurant my friend led me to that day. The place was microscopic, with two or three tables inside and a few more crammed on the sidewalk. Its facade was unremarkable, bearing no distinguishing architectural characteristics whatsoever. My friend's family ate there regularly not because it was charming and trendy, but because the chef had deep, holy knowledge of how to create a mystical, possibly transcendent pupusa. *Ay caramba*, I was not disappointed that day. *Me encantaron esas pupusas.* And I loved my friend for guiding me to the right table to reveal the glory of her native homeland to me.

Just as my native-to-El Salvador friend was the pupusa expert who came to teach me about her family and her native land, allow me to suggest to you that our native-to-the-kingdom-of-God Jesus came to Earth to do us one better: Jesus speaks the language of God and feeds us a holy meal to open our hearts to love his Father for eternity. He had compassion on us, the non-native speakers, so Jesus came to feed us his Father's soul food. Lest I seem to be diminishing Jesus into a random Groupon tour guide service, let's read some of his own words to back up this idea about Jesus as our native divine guide.

In John 16, Jesus was days away from his arrest and death sentence. After three years of teaching in parables, Jesus got specific about what his disciples would need to know after his torture and execution. John said the conversation went like this:

> On that day you will ask in my name, and I am not tell-
> ing you that I will ask the Father on your behalf. For the
> Father himself loves you, because you have loved me
> and have believed that I came from God. I came from
> the Father and have come into the world. Again, I am
> leaving the world and going to the Father."
>
> His disciples said, "Look, now you're speaking
> plainly and not using any figurative language. Now we
> know that you know everything and don't need anyone
> to question you. By this we believe that you came from
> God." (John 16:26–30 CSB)

Here we see the disciples affirm their belief that Jesus is from God. They had been with Jesus for the long haul. They got it—he was a native of heaven, and from then on, they committed to never question Jesus's authority again. For those of us who have been Christians for a while, we might feel the same way. We've been through a lot with Jesus. He's done some cool stuff for us. He's been right about things time and time again. We have the basics about lordship and faith down, and we're ready to move on to debate more intriguing topics, like predestination or the mark of the beast.

Let's bookmark free will and the end times for a good long minute (or the rest of this book) to return to John 16, because Jesus offers us a spiritually vital ingredient here. The rising number of people who have been wounded in communities of faith, the bickering among and polarization of people of faith, and our general need for deconstruction and reconstruction these days all suggest we could benefit from a chef-guided tour through the lordship of Jesus Christ. This shouldn't surprise us. Spiritual growth requires a return to basics, again and again.

Even the disciples present in John 16 would need to be reminded later to take another bite of the truth that Jesus really knew everything and was Lord of everything. A few chapters after our John 16 passage, these same disciples who swore commitment forever gave up on Jesus after his arrest. The disciples' flakiness shows us that reaffirming and submitting to Jesus as Lord and savior is a continual practice in the spiritual life. Receiving Jesus as Lord isn't a one-time decision. Allowing our native divine guide to lead us to unfamiliar and possibly offensive tables is, therefore, inherently part of our spiritual growth.

We should never assume we've got this Jesus as Lord thing all figured out. Figuring everything out with our brains is not the ultimate goal of our spiritual life. The God of the Bible is far less concerned with how much people understand and is more focused on how much they're willing to trust him when understanding is impossible. A keen example of this is in John 16, when the disciples were relieved that Jesus was no longer speaking in parables and when they exuberantly got the most important thing right: Jesus is the Christ! They were thrilled that their brains had arrived at this truth. However, Jesus was not necessarily dazzled by the disciples' new aha moment. He kind of shook his head and let them in on a secret: they would all be scattered and abandon him soon.

> Jesus responded to them, "Do you now believe? Indeed, an hour is coming, and has come, when each of you will be scattered to his own home, and you will leave me alone." (John 16:31–32 CSB)

The disciples finally grasped that Jesus was their native divine guide, but then Jesus informed them that this revelation wasn't ultimately centered on them or what they understood. Jesus clearly didn't need the disciples' votes to be the Messiah. His divine authority and power are independent of people's understanding of it. Therefore, what Jesus said next shouldn't surprise us. When Jesus talked about his best people ghosting him, his chill factor was high.

> Yet I am not alone, because the Father is with me. I have told you these things so that in me you may have peace. You will have suffering in this world. Be courageous! I have conquered the world. (John 16:32–33 CSB)

Jesus basically said something like, *No worries, guys. God's got me, and I'm going to win, so it's all good.* These words of Jesus sound like an influencer's post about the importance of self-confidence when people let you down. What table, exactly, is our native divine guide leading us to with this declaration of a victorious connection to God? We seem to be headed off-road a little with our native divine guide Jesus. If we end up driving off a cliff and then walking on water with him, I hope you're taking a video of it for TikTok.

And just like that, our discussion about Jesus as Lord has led us to a chat about TikTok. As it turns out, the path to the good Jesus stuff requires a peek at lordship in the land of outrageous comments and offensive truth.

Ride or Die with Jesus

TikTok, after all, has ruined us all.

Sorry, am I letting my Gen-X slip show a little too much? Do I sound like an old lady yelling at the neighborhood kids to stay out of her rosebushes? Are you wondering if my middle name is Karen yet?[3]

I'm less of a TikTok hater and more of a recovering social media addict. Puppy videos, challenges that result in someone face-planting into the carpet, and actual footage of elderly couples being reunited after hospitalizations have eroded every responsible bone in my body. I swipe for one more reel and forget who I am, what the meaning of life is, and what I plan to do with the pound of chicken thawing on my countertop.

What I do remember is that I blame TikTok and the delightful content humans create on social media for my easy way of forgetting that Jesus is the most important thing.[4]

Perhaps this forgetfulness is partly due to how chummy we've gotten with Jesus. Don't get me wrong—I adore Jesus. I love his tender, compassionate heart. I am grateful for his grace and mercy. If it weren't for the way Jesus calms my anxious thoughts, I wouldn't

---

[3] My apologies to all the people named Karen. I think you're lovely and wish I could buy you some ice cream. Even though my middle name is *not* Karen, I'd be happy to change it as an act of solidarity.

[4] I love playing the blame game, don't you? It's a glorious way to be self-righteous and smug about our weaknesses and vulnerabilities. Feel free to share this idea with your therapist and let her fix it—later though, okay?

have the courage to roll out from under my warm weighted blanket every morning.

When people talk about Jesus like he's their personal ride or die, I realize they have the gospel a little wonky. Jesus already rode and died. Submitting to the lordship of Christ is our opportunity to prove we grasp the true identity of Jesus. And just who is he, exactly? That question is often inspired by offense and misinformation, which coincidentally makes it like every scathing social media comment we've ever encountered.

Of course, we aren't the first people to ask who Jesus is. There are several instances in Scripture where Jesus's identity was questioned. The Sanhedrin were pretty vigilant about getting an answer from him in Matthew 26. The Samaritan woman in John 4 sort of passive-aggressively asked Jesus who he was when she told him the Messiah was coming. And in Matthew 11:1–6, John the Baptist, who had already proclaimed Jesus as the lamb of God, sent his disciples to question Jesus's identity. They asked Jesus if he was "the one who is to come, or should we expect someone else" (Matt. 11:3 CSB)? Jesus replied, "Go and report to John what you hear and see: The blind receive their sight, the lame walk, those with leprosy are cleansed, the deaf hear, the dead are raised, and the poor are told the good news, and blessed is the one who isn't offended by me" (Matt. 11:4–6 CSB).

This answer from Jesus seems relatively straightforward. Jesus pointed to his miracles and his care for the poor as evidence that he was the Son of God. But the last part is compelling, isn't it? "Blessed is the one who isn't offended by me."[5] Apparently, being the Son of God involves potentially offending people. This statement raises two questions. First, was John offended by Jesus? Given that John was imprisoned at the time (see Mark 6:14–25 for

---

[5] I dare you to make this your bio statement on Twitter.

that juicy story), he was probably at least a little antsy about Jesus getting on with the restoration of all things already. Second, why would Jesus say people are blessed if they aren't offended by him? Or better yet, what's so potentially offensive about who Jesus is?

Let's peek into the possible offense inherent to origin stories to find answers to these questions.

Jesus: The Original Origin Story

Many years ago, my husband, Morgan, had a conversation with our then three-year-old son about a toy. My son brought a small train to him and presented it proudly and said: "My train is from Target."[6]

"That's right. What about your shirt? Where is that from?"

"TAR-get," said the cutest, tiniest little voice ever, as the boy pointed at the dinosaur on his chest.

"And that blanket?" Morgan pointed at a throw on the sofa.

"Tar-GET!" the boy became more enthusiastic every time he realized he knew the answer to the question. Toddlers love to prove they are authorities and masters of information.

"What about you? Where did you come from, buddy?" Morgan asked.

This momentarily stumped the child. But then he realized that everything in our house had come from the same place, and he answered with a question of his own: "I dunno . . . Target??"

As his birth mother, I found it highly offensive that my three-year-old thought he could have been born into this world the same way we bring home a bag of tortilla chips. I gained dozens of pounds while this child marinated in my belly. I bore down and

---

[6] Almost 90 percent of the items in my house were carried in one Target bag at a time. I am a sucker for any establishment where I have access to a full espresso bar, can shop for daily necessities like milk and toilet paper, and where I am also allowed to set a pretty lamp and a new fake leather jacket on a checkout conveyor belt next to a box of Tums.

birthed him with foolish pride, telling the anesthesiologist to get out because I wanted to be the birthing room equivalent of Rambo. I have never been haunted by a Target shopping experience, but I will forever be haunted by the words, "We aren't going to be able to numb you for these stitches," which the doctor spoke after that boy was born.[7]

I mean, I get it. It's cute that he thought he came from Target, but the suggestion was blasphemous from a mother's perspective. And yet, how often have I done the same thing? I've used my own experiences to draw conclusions about myself and Jesus while ignoring his place as the Lord of creation and author of all truth. *Jesus blessed me, so he must love me* and *Jesus isn't answering my prayer because I've disappointed him* are two of the most overused versions of *I came from Target* statements in the whole world. Like John the Baptist, we like to look at our circumstances and assume they reveal the true nature of Jesus. But actually, the truth about Jesus is so potentially offensive, we subconsciously avoid it.

If we read on in Matthew 11, past Jesus's conversation with John the Baptist's disciples, we get a taste of the offensive nature of the truth about Jesus. Jesus told the crowd what a stellar man John was, and then he shifted gears and gave a bit of a lecture about how horrible the people of that generation were. He compared them to children who complain that other children wouldn't play their games the way they wanted them to play. Then Jesus called out the hypocrisy of criticizing John the Baptist for one thing and himself for another. And then, Jesus got big and harsh with his words:

> Then [Jesus] proceeded to denounce the towns where
> most of his miracles were done, because they did not
> repent: "Woe to you, Chorazin! Woe to you, Bethsaida!

---

[7] This was as horrific as it sounds. My husband was oblivious to what was happening because he was checking on the baby, so a stranger held my hand while I cried. Let the record show I deserved some chocolate cake afterward.

For if the miracles that were done in you had been done in Tyre and Sidon, they would have repented in sackcloth and ashes long ago. But I tell you, it will be more tolerable for Tyre and Sidon on the day of judgment than for you. And you, Capernaum, will you be exalted to heaven? No, you will go down to Hades. For if the miracles that were done in you had been done in Sodom, it would have remained until today. But I tell you, it will be more tolerable for the land of Sodom on the day of judgment than for you." (Matt. 11:20–24 CSB)

What happened to Jesus, the tender teacher, who welcomed the little children and had a lovely blue sash over his pristine white robe? Who exactly did Jesus think he was, denouncing the unrepentant? How dare he consider repentance as the only acceptable response to his miracles? Surely there was some kind of "easy grace button" all the people of Chorazin and Bethsaida could have pushed. This speech feels a bit like a slap in the face, only worse because my face is already sunburnt with sin, and the slap caught me off guard because Jesus recently did a miracle for me, which seemed so lovely of him.

Jesus's claim to be Lord isn't offensive until we begin to recognize what it says about us.

Physically speaking, in John 1:1–3, we learn that half of my son's *Target is the source of all matter* worldview was correct. Everything does come from the same place. However, time, matter, and energy aren't from a big-box store with Joanna Gaines licensed merchandise, a subpar Starbucks, and an Icee machine. The Bible says, "In the beginning was the Word, and the Word was with God, and the Word was God. He was with God in the beginning. All things were created through him, and apart from him not one thing was created that has been created" (John 1:1–3 CSB).

As we read on in this passage, we learn that Jesus is the Word. Jesus was in the beginning. He was/is with God, and he was/is God. Everything that exists came from Jesus. He doesn't have an origin story as much as he is the story of the origin of our entire universe. Everything around us that seems like it came from a store came from Jesus. The desk I sit at used to stand tall in a forest, the great-great-great-great-grandchild of a tree Jesus spoke into existence. The gel pen on this desk and the Mason jar that holds that pen were both made from the stuff Jesus had already created: petroleum, sand, and metal.

We live in the physical world where we look for physical evidence of greatness, power, and authority. We easily understand that real flesh-and-blood people figured out how to make a gel pen so that the ink seeps out at just the right quantity to produce a line of ink. We honor the greatness of the people who patented, manufactured, branded, and sold this pen. We forget the powerful creator who made the pen stuff with his Word. Our tendency to live only in awareness of the shallow space of the physical world is what disconnects us from the divine authority of Jesus.

In Acts 17, the apostle Paul took this one step further when he claimed that the authority of Christ is hidden not only in the physical world, but also in every detail of our lives. The details of our existence were not only created by Jesus but were also given a specific purpose—namely, to cause us to reach for Christ.

> From one man he has made every nationality to live over the whole earth and has determined their appointed times and the boundaries of where they live. He did this so that they might seek God, and perhaps they might reach out and find him, though he is not far from each one of us. For in him we live and move and

have our being, as even some of your own poets have
said, "For we are also his offspring." (Acts 17:26–28 CSB)

In Jesus we live. In Jesus we move. In Jesus we have our being.
Everything exists in Jesus.

What does it mean to live *in* Jesus? Should I think of Jesus as
a house we inhabit? If I told you that your being is *in* someone
else, what would that imply about you and about them? If I said
all your real movement is *in* someone, how would that impact
your decisions?

It is beautiful and terrible to realize we exist in Jesus. It is
beautiful because it means we are never alone. But it is terrible
because it means Jesus has the final say about everything we think,
say, or do. And we so often think, say, and do things without much
intentionality or regard for anyone except ourselves and our own
interests, which results in sin.

Paul understood this. He suggested that the solution to our
sin problem was built into God's plan to redeem us. He said the
Son of God came to live as a man for one purpose: to prove that
repentance has been commanded of us because God will one day
judge us all.

> Therefore, having overlooked the times of ignorance,
> God now commands all people everywhere to repent,
> because he has set a day when he is going to judge the
> world in righteousness by the man he has appointed. He
> has provided proof of this to everyone by raising him
> from the dead. (Acts 17:30–31 CSB)

In the Western church, our understanding of the gospel has
long focused on living submitted to Jesus in our personal lives.
Pursuing this doesn't mean we always get it right. We struggle
with how the lordship of Jesus should shape our personal choices

and relationships because the centrality of the lordship of Jesus requires us to consider all the ramifications of Jesus being Lord over all matter, ideas, and innovation. Frankly, it's just a lot to grasp at once. But as Abraham Kuyper said in his speech to open the Free University in Amsterdam in 1880, "There's not a square inch in the whole domain of human existence over which Christ, who is Lord over all, does not exclaim, 'Mine!'"

Jesus is pointing at each of us today and proclaiming us as his. This seems awfully bossy of him, doesn't it? The numerous implications of Jesus as the boss of all of us scramble when I try to run and catch them. How can we keep track of how the lordship of Jesus affects every aspect of our personal lives, careers, relational rhythms, organizational involvements, and larger world issues? It seems like too much, all at once. No wonder so many Christians fight on Facebook about so many things and then go scroll through TikTok to forget the drama.

Are you as exhausted by the thought of chasing all the implications of bossy Jesus as I am? I think I pulled a hammy trying to keep his pace in 2021. What, exactly, does Jesus want to do for us as our Lord (aka boss)? The answer to that lies in a story from Matthew 9, when some men carried a paralytic man to Jesus in the middle of a very religious crowd, and Jesus boiled lordship down to a fairly central theme:

> Just then some men brought to him a paralytic lying on a stretcher. Seeing their faith, Jesus told the paralytic, "Have courage, son, your sins are forgiven."
>
> At this, some of the scribes said to themselves, "He's blaspheming!"
>
> Perceiving their thoughts, Jesus said, "Why are you thinking evil things in your hearts? For which is easier: to say, 'Your sins are forgiven,' or to say, 'Get up and

walk'? But so that you may know that the Son of Man
has authority on earth to forgive sins"—then he told the
paralytic, "Get up, take your stretcher, and go home." So
he got up and went home. When the crowds saw this,
they were awestruck and gave glory to God, who had
given such authority to men. (Matt. 9:2–8 CSB)

This scene scandalized the scribes present that day. In their estimation, Jesus was guilty of blasphemy for implying he could forgive someone's sins. Jesus's miraculous signs had led them all to his proverbial table, but they didn't like what he was serving that day. To them, forgiveness wasn't something a teacher could stick in his back pocket and pass out like lollipops in the Jewish tradition. Before Jesus arrived on the scene, forgiveness was exclusively God's to give. It required a sacrifice at the temple. A priest had to be involved. You couldn't simply have faith and be forgiven, because God's forgiveness was supposed to cost you something.

Instead of healing the paralyzed man as everyone expected that day, Jesus served up a plate of forgiveness for his sins. Jesus was Lord and therefore got to be the boss of what happened next, no matter what the people expected from him. Jesus knew frying forgiveness in hot mercy would make it taste like freedom to the poor in spirit while causing bile to rise in the mouths of the self-righteous leaders. For the scribes, retaining power as the only source of God's forgiveness set them up to receive the sacrifices of the repentant.

What exactly was the bossy Son of God accomplishing in Matthew 9? By prioritizing the forgiveness of a person's sins over their expectation for a physical miracle, Jesus proved three things at once. First, he proved that, as Lord, he is more concerned with our eternal forgiveness than our worldly comfort or healing. Second, Jesus proved that it ought to take more courage to believe God will forgive you than to believe God will heal you. And third, in a culture that assumed your external, physical circumstances were evidence of your internal, spiritual status, Jesus proved that a person could be spiritually whole and right with God yet still have a broken physical circumstance.

All in all, Jesus proved that he was the scribes' boss and that they were wrong about many things that day. They didn't appreciate this at all. So, of course, the scribes branded this teaching as blasphemous fake news. Jesus knew the scribes thought he was blaspheming. I imagine Jesus sort of shrugging and rolling his eyes about their opinions. Then Jesus acquiesced and proved he had the authority to forgive sins by commanding the now-forgiven-but-still-paralyzed man to get up and take his stretcher home. The man obeyed, and the sign caused the crowds to glorify God because God had given such authority to a man. *Oh! He's the boss after all!*

Jesus tried to serve that crowd a truth meal about God's authority, but they refused to lift a single fork at first. They came with hands full of expectations, but they were unwilling to open those hands up and let bossy Jesus put something unexpected in them. I'd love to say that I have no idea what this is like, except, of course, I can't. Jesus has foisted many unexpected circumstances on me through the years. Take, for example, the flight my daughter and I made to Tampa last year.

Jesus, Be the Center (Seat)

In February, my daughter and I boarded a plane to Florida on our way to a dance competition. If you have never taken a dance performance trip, you should know nothing is relaxing or easy about the experience. Dance trips are anxiety marathons.[8] I'm always paranoid that we will forget some essential costume accessory

---

[8] If you watch *Dance Moms*, remember that reality TV is not reality. Real dance trips are about 10 percent like that show.

or the Lipstick She Must Wear. After all, the tragic consequences caused by one girl in the group wearing red lipstick instead of berry lipstick are insurmountable.

Despite packing the correct lipstick, my anxiety was at peak levels when we boarded the plane to Florida. We had already navigated the loss of a ballet shoe, a one-hour flight delay, and an airport dinner that was unexpectedly spicy and therefore inedible for my daughter.[9] Once we found the last two seats on the plane, my expectations were to have a snack and escape into my book for the two-hour flight to Tampa. However, bossy Jesus had a different in-flight meal planned for me.

The excitement began when my daughter asked me to take the middle seat because sitting beside a stranger scared her too much. I was so ~~ticked~~ chill about it.

"Of course, baby. I'll sit in the middle."[10]

Little did I know, my daughter had carried me on a proverbial stretcher to Jesus so God could reveal his authority to me. In my defense, the woman in the window seat looked nothing like an ancient Jewish man or a divine and mighty God, so how was I supposed to know God was about to use her to reveal my blindness and selfishness?

I smiled at window-seat woman as I scooched into my seat.[11] She smiled back and asked if it was my daughter's first flight. I said it wasn't, and then I promptly dug my earbuds out of my purse and

---

[9] How I was able to birth consecutive children of whom the first asks for the hottest sauce possible in which to dip his chips and the next faints at the whiff of mild, I will never know.

[10] No introvert has ever been chill about sitting in the middle seat.

[11] Is there a better word in the English language than *scooch* to describe how anxious people approach forced social interaction? I think not.

opened my book, trusting these items to do the dirty work and communicate my desire to be left alone.[12]

Ten seconds after I put an earbud in, the woman began sobbing into her hands and cursing rather loudly about the passengers on the plane taking too long to find seats.

So I watched Hulu and ignored her for the next two hours while she spiraled into despair. Just kidding! I'm an introvert with mild social anxiety, but I am not a monster.

I (begrudgingly) closed my book and put away my earbuds. Then I (hesitantly) reached out and (screamed inside while I) put my hand on the woman's shoulder and offered to pray for her. After I prayed, I (physically ached to escape into my book, but instead) listened to all the sad stories she was carrying.

Her name was Jackie. Her mom's name was Betty. Betty was very sick, and Jackie was afraid her mom would die before she got to her. Before takeoff, this woman had poured her heart out to me using extremely colorful language. This made more sense when she confided in me that she had eased some of her pain with a drink or eight at the airport bar. When Jackie apologized for how poorly she was coping, I assured her that everyone struggles sometimes. We made small talk after that, which is to say that I died a few more deaths as we discussed things that didn't seem important at all. At the end of the flight, Jackie reached under her seat and pulled out an empty sandwich box from a takeout place.

"Is this yours?" she asked.

"Um, no," I said.[13]

---

[12] My personality cocktail of introversion, social anxiety, and an extreme dislike for small talk make unassigned seating on planes a holy terror for me. Southwest Airlines must have been invented by extreme extroverts.

[13] I wasn't sure how she thought I had secretly eaten an entire sandwich since we had been two inches away from one another for two hours. Jackie will probably be a mystery in my life for as long as I live.

"So, I'm holding someone's trash from an earlier flight?"

"I guess so," I said.

Jackie shrugged and took the old garbage with her when she left. I never saw her again, but I thought about Jackie and Betty many times that week. I thought about God's clear message to my sinful, self-centered self: that I exist to offer his love and care to hurting people, not to disappear into my book and music after a hectic afternoon.

You never really know what you're going to get with bossy Jesus. Sometimes he gives you a friend who leads you to the best pupusas in Los Angeles. Sometimes he gives you a grieving seat-mate with random rubbish and no concept of personal space. The tricky part is figuring out what to do once you reach out and grasp that Jesus can use both people to reveal himself as Lord to you.

Here in the unpredictable, mysterious days of our lives, amid bright days and dark nights, we live and move and exist in Jesus, the boss of us. Jesus is the foremost authority in charge of our classmates' lunch plans. He is on our flights to Tampa. As a matter of fact, Jesus reigns supreme in every moment of our day. When we reach out and fully grasp him as Lord, we're ready to open our hands to more complicated questions, like what does it mean to be friends with the Lord of all? Can we really be friends with the boss of the universe?

To move into that question, let's check out what Jesus said about friendship in John 15. I like friendship, don't you? Friendship is pretty great. In a head-to-head race, it even gives pupusas a run for their money.

CHAPTER

Jesus

as Our Mysterious BFF

"Oh, I wish I could, but I don't want to."

—Phoebe Buffay,[1] when asked to help assemble Ross's furniture

*F*riendship can be a real mystery sometimes.[2] Even more mysterious are these words of Jesus: "You are my friends if you do what I command you" (John 15:14 CSB). They make me want to bake a loaf of banana bread and knock on Jesus's door to ask him to break down the connection between commands and friendship, because when it comes to understanding friendship with the Lord of all, I feel like I'm looking at a *Where's Waldo?* book while blindfolded.

The mysterious topic of friendship and Jesus reminds me of a distant time when my now-giant-adult son was much shorter than

---

[1] *Friends*, season 1, episode 1, "The One Where Monica Gets a Roommate," aired September 2, 1994, on NBC.

[2] I'm not just talking about the way the middle school lunchroom and/or locker room came to attack every human being's self-confidence once upon a time.

I am and attended preschool. At the beginning of every school day, the preschool director presented a mystery box to the children and asked them a series of questions to solve the mystery.

"What do you think could be in the box?" Ms. Diana would ask the children.

Those four-year-olds relished guessing what was in the box. *A book! A peanut! My mom's lipstick!* After a dozen wrong guesses, Ms. Diana would open the box and show the class the item she had chosen for the day.

"What is it?" Ms. Diana asked the second question.

This was even better than guessing for the children. This was their chance to prove they really knew something. Hands eagerly shot up all around the room. Ms. Diana would choose a child to proudly name the item. Generally, the mystery box housed an ordinary object from Ms. Diana's house or yard. I'm not sure there was a lot of thought put into the mystery box's thing. I often wondered if Ms. Diana absentmindedly grabbed a leaf, a screwdriver, or an envelope on her way out the door. Whatever the box held, it was a recognizable object every child could identify. Despite how easy the task was, the child chosen named the thing with great pride.

"It's a coffee cup," the child would say, nodding and looking at everyone to make sure anyone who had never seen a coffee cup before now grasped what the group was dealing with today.

Once identified, Ms. Diana always asked the same two questions next. First, she would ask, "What does it do? What is it good for?" Then, after the children explained that a coffee cup held hot liquids, helped their parents wake up, or could even be used to grow a tiny plant, Ms. Diana asked the last question to help us all grasp the divine mystery a little better: "How is this coffee cup like God?"

I have an entire school of preschool-aged theologians to thank for showing me that God is like a coffee cup because he holds us to keep us warm, he is good at waking us up, and he can grow beautiful things. They taught me that God is like an envelope because he is full of important information and because he sends us to people to tell them important messages. They proved unequivocally that God is like a bouncy ball because he makes us happy when we hold him and he is fun to share with other people. Kids are wiser than we expect and are more aware of God than our standard-issue adult cynicism allows us to be at any given moment of our day.

I'd like to play the part of Ms. Diana today and pull friendship out of the mystery box so we can better understand what it can teach us about Jesus. I'd also like to consider what our friendship with Jesus can teach us about one another. Frankly, ever since Jenny Blackwood[3] looked at me in the fourth grade and said I couldn't sit with her at lunch anymore, I've been aware that friendship can get spicy and complicated. Friends say crazy stuff and do crazy things that mystify us. Our dearest, favorite people let us down and expect too much of us, time and time again. This is true of our IRL friends and our divine friend, Jesus.

Since I married my best friend, spicy friendship has been a constant theme in our marital life. We've been pulling each other out of the mystery box for twenty years now and asking, *Who are you? What did you do? And how in the world can I learn who Jesus is from this relationship?!*

One of these first mystery box moments happened about a year after our wedding when Morgan and I took a trip to Idaho to celebrate his grandparents' fiftieth wedding anniversary. I had met his grandparents at our wedding, but our interaction was brief, and I made a massive blunder after the ceremony. Morgan's

---

[3] Blessings to you, wherever you are, Jenny B. I'm sorry I was so jealous of your name-brand Doritos and real Oreos. #mymomboughtgeneric

grandmother approached with congratulatory love, but I mistook her for her sister Elsie, a fellow wedding guest.

"Hi, Aunt Elsie!" I sort of shouted and cheered these words because I was a lunatic bride who was very introverted, and social interaction in large crowds turns me into a frenetic Spice Girl.[4]

"This is my *grandmother*," Morgan side-eyed me. All he had expected of me as his friend at that moment was to memorize his grandmother's face, and I had failed to meet this expectation.

Grammie was sweet about the blunder, saying she and Elsie looked similar. I appreciated the grace and forgot all about my faux pas as the night went on.

But as we headed to Idaho for the anniversary weekend, the mistake of my past haunted me. Being Morgan's best friend meant trying to fit in and be relaxed around his extended family. However, overthinking my wedding-day failure seemed like the best and most dysfunctional game plan for the weekend.[5] So I went with it.

We flew into Boise, and Morgan's grandparents picked us up at the airport. The stories about riding in a car with Gramps are family lore. Gramps was a retired Marine colonel, and riding in his car through freeway traffic was akin to being a jeep passenger amid jungle combat.

Lanes were *suggestions* to Gramps. He liked to make eye contact with everyone in the backseat while directing our vision toward points of interest. Gramps fought in multiple wars and survived bullets and bombs countless times; he certainly wasn't going to let Patty in her Corolla threaten him.

I liked riding with Gramps. His fearless grit made space for me to hope we could all put the Grammie/Elsie fiasco behind us.[6]

---

[4] I don't think either Aunt Elsie or Grammie wanted to zig-a-zig-ah.

[5] At the ripe age of twenty-six, I was super whole on the inside.

[6] No one else remembered it even happened. Most of my insecurities exist only in my head. It would take another twenty years of overthinking for me to grasp this fully.

However, things got complicated again when we got to Gramps and Grammie's house. All the out-of-town siblings and grandchildren would be staying in the house together. They were super excited, but I was just super nervous and anxious about finding a way to blend in to the large group and their boisterous familial activities.

Gramps had his own concerns about the number of people under his roof. The house's plumbing utilized a septic system that usually only supported the water usage of two people. There would be a dozen extra people showering, using toilets, and washing dishes there now. Gramps lined us up and gave us our orders.

"Navy showers, everyone. You have two minutes, in and out. Conserve water as much as possible. We don't want to have to call a septic company this weekend."

I was terrified of getting demerits for using too much water, but I had never timed my showers in my life. I had no idea how to strategize my efforts in there. I assumed no one let their hair conditioner soak into their hair for a minute in the Navy. But even if I didn't use conditioner, how would I wash my body, shave my legs, and shampoo my hair in two minutes? I also assumed being in the Navy required cold showers because it takes more than a minute for the hot water to get to you.[7] I did my best to be a good soldier, but I can't confirm the duration of my time in the shower. I went as fast as I could. Mostly.

The septic tank backed up the next day. No one blamed me to my face. *Selah.*[8]

Gramps called the septic company and set up his fifth wheel in the driveway to use as a bathroom while plumbers resolved the situation.

---

[7] I am so glad I never joined the Navy.

[8] I plead the fifth. I didn't have a watch back then, and there were no smartphones to time my shower. I have no idea how long it took me in that shower.

Have you ever taken a shower in a tiny camper? Remember that scene from the movie *Elf* when giant human-sized Buddy is in the small elf-sized shower splashing little handfuls of water on his shoulders? A camper shower is like that, except smaller.

But before I could get into the tiny shower, I had to carry all my clothes and toiletries through the house, past rooms full of strangers who were now my family. Then I had to take my dirty clothes and toiletries back to our room while simultaneously announcing the shower was now available for the next person. Public declarations of my bathroom usage shattered my plan to fly beneath the social radar.

Given my marital vows and my love for Morgan, I couldn't just dip out and head to Motel 6 for the week. My experiences with Morgan's family are evidence of one of the most important truths about friendship: when we choose a friend, they come attached to other people.

Friendly in a Crowd with Jesus

A big part of friendship is loving the people already attached to your new friend. This is true for regular flesh-and-blood friends and divine, holy friends. Friendship with Jesus is a package deal. After all, he comes to us already attached to the Father, the Holy Spirit, and the whole world he created. Let's return to John 15 to hear Jesus talk more about friendship with him:

> This is my command: Love one another as I have loved
> you. No one has greater love than this: to lay down his
> life for his friends. You are my friends if you do what
> I command you. I do not call you servants anymore,
> because a servant doesn't know what his master is doing.
> I have called you friends, because I have made known
> to you everything I have heard from my Father. You

did not choose me, but I chose you. I appointed you to
go and produce fruit and that your fruit should remain,
so that whatever you ask the Father in my name, he
will give you. This is what I command you: Love one
another. (John 15:12–17 CSB)

It is both a beautiful truth and the central theme of the gospel that
our friendship with Jesus means we're in the cool kids' club with
God the Father and God the Holy Spirit. After all, Jesus came to lay
down his life to atone for our sin so we could be reunited with the
whole triune God. But in John 15, Jesus explained there are other
strings attached to our choice to accept his offer of friendship. Do
you feel a fresh burn when you read in context the "you are my
friends if you do what I command you" bit in Jesus's friendship
explanation?[9] Our BFF Jesus expects us to obey his command to
love . . . other people.

Just as befriending Morgan meant taking bumpy rides with
Gramps, making awkward apologies to Grammie, and hunkering down in cold RV showers, our friendship with Jesus may
involve some uncomfortable interactions with the other people
in Jesus's life.

Who, exactly, is included in this "one another" group Jesus
commanded us to love here in John 15? Is it possible he meant we
ought to love the cleaned-up, friendly people who are so easy to
adore? Is the crowd around Jesus full of holy saints who will love
us in return? Well, since Romans 5:8 (CSB) famously reports that
"God proves his own love for us in that while we were still sinners,
Christ died for us," it's safe to say Jesus doesn't consider a person's
holiness or righteousness a prerequisite for love. But just to be

---

[9] Let us bow our heads in submission as we are reminded afresh that Jesus is a
bossy friend.

sure, let's take a closer look at the kind of people Jesus befriended during his life on Earth.

Who's in the Friend Zone

The first friends Jesus chose to hang out with when he began his public ministry were nobodies. In Matthew 4, Jesus found two sets of brothers out fishing. Jesus first told Simon and Andrew, and then James and John, that he could make them fishers of people. It seems unlikely that these four men sat around dreaming of fishing for people on the regular. However, the more detailed account of this story in John 5 reveals a miraculous load of fish brought in after they obeyed Jesus and threw their nets out one more time. The empty lake suddenly produced so many fish that their nets broke and their boats began to sink. This miracle drew all four men out of the still waters of their ordinary lives. They were never the same again.

Jesus chose regular, workaday people to be his first friends and followers. He didn't find political leaders or inspirational rabbis full of power or charisma. These men didn't have connections to help a revolutionary leader overturn the status quo. Jesus walked up to ragged, tired fishermen and said, *You're the friends I want in my life. Do what I say, and I'll blow your mind.*

Take that truth to the bank when you feel like a hidden nobody. Read John 5 when you feel pressured to be more influential, successful, or better connected in life. Shove this story in the hole of your soul when you think God only chooses famous or flawlessly beautiful people to change the world. Jesus has invited our ordinary, faithful selves into his inner circle.

Jesus also likes to mix things up when he chooses his friends. Those four fishermen seem like much safer choices compared with the next person Jesus invited into his inner circle. In John 5:27–31, Jesus asked Levi, an oppressive and crooked tax collector, to be his friend. This was scandalous because tax collectors were Jewish men who helped Rome oppress the Jewish people. These cultural sellouts often took advantage of their Rome-backed authority to gouge even more money from their fellow Jews.

As it turned out, Levi was popular in his circles. The Bible says he hosted a big banquet, and the number of tax collectors in attendance scandalized the religious leaders. The scribes and Pharisees complained about their presence. Luke 5:31–32 (csb) says, "Jesus replied to them, 'It is not those who are healthy who need a doctor, but those who are sick. I have not come to call the righteous, but sinners to repentance.'"

Jesus made good on this promise later in the Gospels when he befriended prostitutes and adulterers, touched unclean people, ate at the house of a leper, and let women sit and listen to his teachings the way only men were usually allowed to do. Jesus, the Son of God, gathered all kinds of people as his friends. This is all fine and good from the distance of a couple thousand years and a different culture. But let's connect the dots from life back then to our own modern lives.

Jesus is best buddies with our boring neighbors who only want to talk about work and grocery shopping. He came to befriend the people who have used and abused us. Jesus is friends with conspiracy theorists and Facebook bullies. His dinner guests tonight are the church leaders who were awful to us, and he wants us to sit next to them. Jesus sits and eats with the people in that other political party who believe crazy stuff about the Bible and refuse to listen to us when we try to explain our perspective.

Jesus enjoys boring people and sketchy characters. He's here for the outrageous and the ordinary. Not everyone we dislike or every person who makes us uncomfortable will accept the invitation and follow Jesus, of course. But when Jesus chooses his friends, he isn't afraid to scrape what we consider the bottom of the barrel. It's even possible someone else finds you and me to be some folks Jesus dredged up from the murky barrel bottom.

Why have so many people over the centuries been willing to leave their whole lives behind to befriend Jesus? Are there bright and shiny perks to being a friend of the Son of God? How is friendship with Jesus worth enduring all the weirdos who show up at his table? I suppose since Jesus is all about healing sick people and feeding the hungry and explaining life and God so beautifully, many of his friends have had expectations that he'll toss them a bone or two when they need it. However, as we'll see next, while Jesus may open his arms to all kinds of odd friends, he doesn't always give us what we expect.

Jesus, the Unpredictable Friend

The famous story of Lazarus's death and resurrection is also about how strange it can be to be Jesus's friend. Before Lazarus died, Mary and Martha sent a message to Jesus to tell him that his beloved friend was sick. Jesus's response is fascinating:

> When Jesus heard it, he said, "This sickness will not
> end in death but is for the glory of God, so that the Son
> of God may be glorified through it." Now Jesus loved
> Martha, her sister, and Lazarus. So when he heard that
> he was sick, he stayed two more days in the place where
> he was. (John 11:4–6 CSB)

At first, Jesus's first response to the sisters' ancient telegram is encouraging. Lazarus wouldn't die, and God would be glorified through Lazarus's sickness. We can all get behind this faith proclamation. *Yes! Lazarus is going to live!* But then the Bible tells us two things that seem contradictory. First, it asserts that Jesus loved Mary, Martha, and Lazarus. And then it says he didn't go to be with them for two more days. During those two days, Lazarus died. It seemed like Jesus had been wrong about the end of his friend's sickness.

Once Jesus arrived in Bethany, the home of Lazarus, Mary, and Martha, it was clear that expectations had already been established in Mary and Martha's minds. Martha greeted Jesus in John 11:21 (CSB) and said, "Lord, if you had been here, my brother wouldn't have died." Then Mary came to him and said, "Lord, if you had been here, my brother wouldn't have died" (John 11:32 CSB)! It's like the sisters had pulled Jesus out of the mystery box and answered the question *What does our friend do?* with *Our friend Jesus heals people.* Mary and Martha expected a miraculous end to Lazarus's illness. But unpredictable Jesus hadn't come, and unimaginable grief had evicted their miraculous expectations.

Let's take a moment to consider the implications. As we suffer and wait for Jesus to answer our prayers for help, this story offers us a hopeful truth about what it means to be friends with Jesus. Our friend Jesus's unmistakable presence and timely response is not the metric we should use to measure his love for us. Jesus deeply loved his friends in John 11, *and* he didn't go to them right away when they wanted him to come. As we saw in the last chapter, Jesus doesn't always do what we expect him to do. Our friend Jesus will disappoint us sometimes while loving us deeply.

The mourners witnessed the great love Jesus had for Lazarus after his conversation with Mary. In John 11:35–36, Jesus wept for his friend Lazarus. I imagine he cried for all the suffering Lazarus, Mary, and Martha went through in the days leading to Lazarus's death. But since Jesus knew he himself would face death and a tomb shortly, I often wonder if Jesus also wept for the grief they would experience in the days ahead.

While we can't always predict the way Jesus will arrive and meet our needs, we can rely on him to be tender and compassionate toward us. He may delay his coming. He may have a plan to rescue us, heal us, and resurrect us long after we expect our miracle. But Jesus is not insensitive toward us, and he mourns and grieves the pain we endure in life—because that's what friends do for one another.

Christianity is the only religion that claims God offers us himself in friendship. We must diligently seek God's wisdom and Word to hold both truths together: that Jesus is our Lord/the boss of us and that he is the fulfillment of Proverbs 18:24, the friend who is closer to us than a devoted brother. But if you recall, the call to love and obey Jesus involves loving one another as well. Hidden in our love for one another is a powerful piece of the mystery of friendship with Jesus. Let's peek inside the mystery box again to see how our personal friendships with one another reveal Jesus to us.

All about the One Another

When I think of the friends God has added to my life, our friends Brett, Melissa, Kevin, and Jody are at the top of my list. Once upon a time, we were all new to living in Austin, and we barely knew each other. Morgan and I had just bought our first house,[10] and there were several empty lots near us. Brett, Morgan, and Kevin all worked in the same office, and when I saw Jody and Melissa at the office Christmas party, I convinced them to buy houses on our street.

I still cannot explain what came over me that day. I barely knew these women; but I blame my weird big-crowd-equals-obnoxious-Spice-Girl behavior again. The words just blurted out, "You should be our neighbors!"

---

[10] Remember when they gave out all those zero-down loans to people in the early 2000s? You know, the ones that broke the economy a few years later? We were one of those loans. #whoops #jesusbeamortgagepayment

Rational Jody thought I needed to calm down. Sweet Melissa couldn't wait to borrow sugar from me and whip up a pan of cookies. My Mister-Rogers-inspired won't-you-be-my-neighbor sales pitch was a hallmark of that Christmas party.

Only the Holy Spirit knows exactly why these friends bought houses on our street. The next few years were glorious. We ate Thanksgiving dinner in June, just for kicks. We painted each other's dining rooms and called each other with warnings about door-to-door salespeople trying to sell vacuums or meat in bulk.[11] We were all simultaneously pregnant with our first babies, and I got to be the videographer when Jody was in labor because I happened to stop by her hospital room at just the right time.[12]

We all eventually moved away from our beloved street when new job offers and more babies came our way. But I still send them the MLS listings on my new street because hope, our friendship, and my weirdness all burn eternal.[13]

Kevin, Jody, Brett, Melissa, Morgan, and I are stuck with each other for the rest of our lives. We have held one another for over twenty years now. Along the way, we've let go of annoyances, frustrations, misunderstandings, and unhealthy expectations of one another.

A few years ago, Kevin and Jody visited with their three kids to celebrate the publication of my first book. Brett and Melissa made the two-mile pilgrimage with their four kids to our house to hang out. Around dinnertime, we realized we had no plan to feed all seventeen of us.[14] I scoured the fridge and, of course, found

---

[11] Morgan's response to bulk meat: *No thanks. Unnecessary responsibility.* Brett's response: *Let's share this meat with everyone we know.* Kevin's response: *I'll take two cows, and please also sell me a deep freezer.*

[12] Jody just kept pointing at her face and yelling at me the whole time, "Keep the camera pointed *up here*, Carrie!!" Jody can be bossy like Jesus.

[13] Please move back onto my street, Kevin and Jody, Brett and Melissa. I miss us.

[14] I had to count how many of us there were because I didn't know. But I was like, *seventeen??* Gosh, that's a lot of kids. No wonder we're so tired.

taco fixings. The kids swarmed the spread immediately. I briefly feared all the cheese would be gone before the adults ate one taco.[15] Once we banished the teenagers to eat in another room and filled our plates, Melissa took a bite of the spicy ground beef that night and said, "I know you use the same ingredients I use when I make this, but for some reason, your taco meat tastes better than mine."

Someone made a corny joke about how it tasted better because I add love to it. They were not wrong. I love all sixteen of those people so much that I prefer to cook for them than go out to eat just to keep them in my house for a few more hours. I stock up on more snacks than we think eleven kids will eat when they're all here, and then those kids empty the pantry and demand more anyway. I never mind when those same kids track dirt through the house playing some weird game of tag called "cops and robbers" that they made up years ago.

I bake lemon blueberry muffins for Kevin because they make him happy. I buy Jody's favorite tea because I want to sit in the early morning hours and listen to her stories about vacuuming and yelling at basketball referees. I stock my fridge with Fuji apples because Brett and Melissa's kids inherited some of my weirdness through osmosis and will only eat Fujis. I dish a double serving of dessert for Brett because Melissa always declines a serving and "just wants a bite of Brett's."[16]

When Melissa said my taco meat tasted better than hers, I knew it was because our love for one another is expert-level after all these years. The food tasted better because Kevin and Jody drove three hours to celebrate with us. It tasted better because Brett and Melissa ran home for a three-pound Costco-size bag of shredded cheese to ensure there would be a handful left when

---

[15] Kids love cheese in profound abundance. This only proves kids are more intelligent than they sometimes seem.

[16] Melissa eats more than a bite of Brett's.

the adults made their tacos. That taco meat was delicious because all our teenagers sacrificed the time they could have spent doing homework and chores to be with us.[17] Life was richer and better that night because Morgan and I threw our introverted tendencies out the window and opened the door to the people we love.

When I went fishing for people to be my neighbors at a Christmas party in 2002, I never could have imagined what lay ahead for all of us. But I can see now that friendship is how Jesus makes us fishers of people. Faithfully loving the people God brings to us is the most evangelistic thing most of us will ever do in life. Jesus, the ultimate authority in the universe, knew this when he commanded us to love one another as he has loved us. We are his friends when we do what he commands because he is love, and friendship is the work of love in the world. Jesus knew that our efforts to sacrificially love one another would change our lives and the world by making all of us fishers of people. But Jesus didn't only command us to love one another to give our lives purpose or improve the status quo.

Friendship with one another is our best chance to open the box and hold the mystery of Jesus with our own two hands. We better grasp what our friendship with Jesus is supposed to entail as we love the ordinary and the outrageous about each other and believe the best about unreliable people. When we stand by one another as our existential septic tank backs up, we remind each other that this is how Jesus loved the world—with his arms spread wide to do whatever necessary to love everyone in need of a cosmic shower. Just as Ms. Diana knew that four-year-olds could find God and his purpose in the world by looking at a coffee cup, Jesus knew we could see him and his purpose if we took some time

---

[17] This is a joke. They welcomed the opportunity to skip their responsibilities and instead demolish my house.

to look at each other long enough to hear him ask us, *How is your love for one another like my love for you?*

We need that question here in the twenty-first century, a time in which no one has lived and breathed and followed Jesus in real life. Jesus commanded his followers to love one another because he knew that, eventually, the people following him wouldn't be those who had face-to-face friendships with him. We didn't eat the multiplied fish and bread. We never walked in the room to see his face light up as he greeted us. We didn't hear him cry out to God on the cross to forgive us all because we didn't know what we were doing. We didn't look into an empty tomb or put our fingers in the scars on his hands and feet. But when we experience friendship together, we get as close as we can to what Jesus's IRL friends experienced: the kind of powerful friendship that inspired them to leave everything behind and follow the Messiah off the beaten path and into the wild, unpredictable terrain of lordship.

Come to think of it, obeying Jesus's call to love as he loved is an awful lot like a ride in Gramps's car. It requires a lot of trust in Jesus, who handles the friendship bus a little like an army jeep. We hold on to one another as he points to the thought-provoking and vital lessons we pass by; and when Jesus looks us in the eye, we must do our best to ignore how close we veer toward the edge of the road.

Like Gramps, Jesus has a specific destination for our road trip, and that's what we'll talk about in the next chapter. There's a lot of love in his spicy friendship sauce; and mostly, it just tastes like home.

Jesus
as Our True Home

"I want to go home."

—Me, any time I'm in public

A few years ago, there was a "Jesus is my homeboy" meme going around on social media. Most of the people posting this and laughing about it were not, in fact, people who had ever once used the word *homeboy* at any prior time in their life. There's nothing more charming than a bunch of people using slang they don't really understand in a reach for increased cool factor, don't you think? Just ask any teenager in the world how they feel when their parents incorporate slang words into their daily language, and it's clear the line between cringe and cool is quite fine.[1]

---

[1] To really bless your teenage children, use lots of slang around their friends. Try this one the next time your house is full of high schoolers: "You guys can call me Bruno Mars 'cause I be drippin' in finesse." (You are welcome.)

But it isn't only teenagers who disdain fakers trying to pass as something they aren't. We all crave authenticity and genuineness from people. This brings me back to the idea of Jesus being someone's homeboy. A "homeboy" or "homegirl" is generally a person from your neighborhood or town, someone you're close to, who shares your same roots and connections. As much as I agree with the sentiment that Jesus wants to be our close friend (as per the previous chapter), unless we grew up on the mean streets of Nazareth, he is not from our neighborhood or our hometown. Jesus is not our homeboy. However, Jesus does, in fact, want to be something special to us. He wants to be our home. How do I know this is true? Well, he makes this offer in John 15:

> Remain in me, and I in you. Just as a branch is unable to produce fruit by itself unless it remains on the vine, neither can you unless you remain in me. I am the vine; you are the branches. The one who remains in me and I in him produces much fruit, because you can do nothing without me. If anyone does not remain in me, he is thrown aside like a branch and he withers. They gather them, throw them into the fire, and they are burned. If you remain in me and my words remain in you, ask whatever you want and it will be done for you. (John 15:4–7 CSB)

The Greek word for *remain* in this passage also can be translated as *abide* or *dwell*. We've talked about how Jesus is the source of creation and therefore reigns as Lord over creation. We've peeked into the mystery of how Jesus relates to us as his friends. But ultimately, to understand the authentic wonder of Jesus, we must see how even though Jesus isn't our homeboy, he is our true home.

Homebodies United

I admit I am a bit of a homebody. I like the familiarity and safety of the space where I abide with the people who love me most in the world. Whenever we travel, I miss my coffeemaker in the morning. Hotel sofas are torture devices compared to the comfort of the spot where I sit and read in my living room. No bed in any vacation home ever soothes me like my own memory foam mattress adorned with my silk-encased pillows and the weighted blanket that is far too heavy to take on a plane. Even so, when I have the chance to leave my home in Texas to visit the place where I grew up, my heart's cry is always the same: "I'm going home."

A few summers ago, before my parents moved out of my childhood home, we packed suitcases and hopped on a plane to California. In my mind, we were going home. For my Texan husband and children, it was a nice trip west.

During that week, I hiked up California hills, reveled in ocean breezes, and welcomed the scent of eucalyptus trees and fresh-cut, year-round-green lawns. I walked to my old elementary school bus stop, just for kicks. I took my kids on a tour of the neighborhood to show them the circa 1982 public walkway/slab of cement with my footprints and the name "Carrie" hastily (and illegally) scribbled in it.[2] My cement art exhibit stood as evidence of my youthful frivolity and proof that place was once *my* place. California was and is this homebody's homiest place. If I could take you on a tour of my soul, you'd find a cement path with the shape of California's feet and the words "I wish they all could be California girls" dug in beside it. Even though I don't live in California any longer, California will always live in me.

---

[2] Many thanks to the state of California for not noticing my penchant for vandalism at the young age of six.

I'm pretty sure this describes what Jesus was aiming at when he commanded us to abide and remain in him as he abides and remains in us. In John 15:7, he made the incredible promise that if we remain in him and his words remain in us, God the Father will do anything we ask of him. I've heard a lot of people shoot this passage down over the years because they think the idea that God will answer any prayer with a giant thumbs up is a little dangerous. *Don't get your hopes up,* they seem to say, *Jesus isn't a golden ticket to whatever you want.* And, in a way, I understand what they're getting at. But I also believe Jesus meant this as a truth we can hold as evidence that making Christ our home affords us some divine privileges.

If it pays to be a Jesus homebody, how do we move in and set up house?

Cleaning Up: A Holy Privilege

When we arrived back at our (real) Texas home after that trip to California, my young children all scattered to their rooms to reacquaint themselves with their familiar toys and games. The silence was a golden thing after the many complaints and arguments generated during our long travel day. I sat at the kitchen table to write out a grocery list, and Morgan carried our luggage back into our bedroom. His voice shattered the quiet house. "Carrie! We have a problem!"

We did, indeed, have a problem. A thunderstorm had flooded our bedroom while we were out of town. The floor was squishy with water that had seeped in under the wall and windows behind our bed. The walls had become sponges, and our furniture was ruined, so we moved into our guest room while the damage was assessed. A few days later, we learned that our insurance didn't cover any of the necessary repairs. And as it turned out, there was a lot to repair.

When we removed the ruined thirty-year-old drywall behind our bed, we discovered the flood was caused by the total deterioration of the studs behind the sheetrock. Two-by-fours had eroded into dust and nothing. The windows sat on air, apparently, without any adequate structural support. On the opposite wall, the improperly poured foundation had allowed even more water in the room. We faced the brutal fact that our house desperately needed a renovation. Before we could set up a new bed and install new flooring, we had to cut away everything rotted and repair the inadequate structural components.

The Word of God can do similar renovation work in our lives. Jesus said, "If you remain in me and my words remain in you, ask whatever you want and it will be done for you" (John 15:7 CSB). It's essential to grasp that abiding in Jesus involves God's Word within us. In Hebrews 4, we read about the incredible potency of God's Word and what it's specifically capable of accomplishing:

> For the word of God is living and effective and sharper
> than any double-edged sword, penetrating as far as the
> separation of soul and spirit, joints and marrow. It is
> able to judge the thoughts and intentions of the heart.
> No creature is hidden from him, but all things are naked
> and exposed to the eyes of him to whom we must give
> an account. (Heb. 4:12–13 CSB)

Consider the truth that God's Word is like a sharp and precise renovation tool living inside us. It cuts and carves away any part of us in need of correction and redemption. The Word of God slices through what we cannot see (soul and spirit), as well as what we can see (bone and marrow). God's Word can fix/heal our souls and our bodies by first showing us the cause of the damage. It carves windows for us to see out of from our own experiences and how those experiences have worn us down to nothing over the years. Those windows let in light so we can see God more clearly. The Word of God can open the walls of our souls so we can face the damage and trauma we've suffered. Once our thoughts and choices lay bare before God's truth, we're free to learn spiritual disciplines to keep our spiritual house clean and in working order. We have space to seek therapy and incorporate wise counsel from trusted people. But it isn't only our souls that need the sharp tool of God's Word. Our bodies are also given greater life and health when God's Word abides in us. When we pray for physical healing, for God to give wisdom to our doctors, and for God to heal our minds of the dysfunctional patterns of addiction or negative self-talk, we stand on the promise of Hebrews 4:12.

Let's not forget as we speak of God's Word that, as we read in John 1 two chapters ago, Jesus is the Word made flesh. To abide in Jesus as he described it in John 15, we dwell in the power of the Word made flesh, and the Word made flesh dwells within us. We are cocooned by and filled with the omnipotent presence of love. No wonder Jesus said anyone who abides in him can ask for anything and it will be done for her. When we make our home in Christ, we have the Word of God, the Lord of all things, the most supreme love and light in the universe available to answer any external or internal need we might have. How could we lack anything?

The tricky part of learning how to abide in Jesus is garnering the courage to pick up the sharp edge of God's Word to let it do its deep work in us. Pointing a holy, spiritual knife at your most profound need can be a terribly vulnerable space. I know this from personal experience.

Orange Skies, Smiling at Me

Many years ago, when I was a college student trying to figure out my life, I held some broken ideas about myself and my life. I was plagued by my imperfection, and my favorite hobby was ruminating on my flaws. I let my fear tell me who I was, and I never bothered to question the negative self-talk in my own head.

A friend of mine, Suzanne, learned this about me, and she challenged me to make a list of my negative attributes and then take that list and use it to create a new list of Bible scriptures that could replace my negativity with hope, grace, and faith. Suzanne knew God's Word was the key to abiding in Jesus. Personally, I thought seeing all my failures and self-doubts spelled out clearly on paper was an excellent idea![3] It would be like celebrating Christmas and my birthday all in one fell swoop.

A month later, Suzanne asked me if my list was making a difference, and I proudly reported that progress was minimal since I never made the list. My negative experiences, feelings, and thoughts felt so true, I didn't want to replace them with what seemed like pie-in-the-sky faith that God loved me no matter what. Who wanted to be the wimp who needed God because she couldn't save herself with her own performance? Not this girl, that's for sure.

"I don't want to walk outside and look at an orange sky and call it blue just because the Bible says it's blue. That sounds ridiculous," I told her.

"If God says the orange sky is blue, call it blue," Suzanne said.

Suzanne understood how filling our hearts and minds with the Word of God cuts out the broken debris of life and removes our self-centered, sinful ways. She knew that our determination to believe in and obey the truth spoken by God is how space is created for God to abide in us and for us to abide in God. God's Word is how we set up house and abide in Jesus.

---

[3] No, I did not.

Abiding in Jesus also offers us a privilege that involves no sharp edges whatsoever. I'm exceedingly confident you'll like this feature of Jesus as our home.

Welcome Home to Divine Confidence

I've never considered myself a naturally confident person. This statement seems true until I recall my early elementary years. I was a boss when I was six, seven, and eight years old. Unstoppable. Borderline obnoxious with my confidence. I raised my hand to answer every question. I wanted to be captain of every team. My whole life was spent jumping up and down, shouting, "Put me in, Coach! I can do it! You'll be so glad you picked me!" The world existed for one purpose: so I could be a part of the action.

What happened, exactly, between the age of eight and eighteen to produce a girl who tiptoed off to college, terrified she didn't have what it took to achieve her dreams?

Well, there are, undoubtedly, many factors that curbed my self-enthusiasm and confidence. Failures humbled me. Mean friends wounded me. My own temperament and wiring solidified, and without ever hearing the word *introvert*, my personality turned inward. But also, cultural messages put asterisks next to much of my confident behavior. Good little girls never behaved in ways that appeared aggressive or contrary to authority figures,[4] and in a grab for goodness and validation, I let go of confidence, along with enthusiasm and liveliness.

To be without self-confidence is to not be at home in your own self because no one sets up residence in a place where they don't believe they can thrive in some way. Likewise, to be without

---

[4] A good prayer for children (and for us!): God, help us not to let how our behavior appears to others define our value or intentions. Gift us with your discernment, and help us to honor and love you, who you made us to be, and others in all we say and do. Amen.

God-confidence is to not be at home in God. When Jesus commanded us to abide and live in him, he offered us a home we could be confident in. John wrote about this in 1 John 4:

> Whoever confesses that Jesus is the Son of God—God remains in him and he in God. And we have come to know and to believe the love that God has for us.
>
> God is love, and the one who remains in love remains in God, and God remains in him. In this, love is made complete with us so that we may have confidence in the day of judgment, because as he is, so also are we in this world. (1 John 4:15–17 CSB)

Love is always the key to greater confidence. To unlock greater confidence in Jesus, we need a deeper understanding of how deeply he loved us. Our confidence in him as a sturdy, safe spiritual home is directly related to our understanding of how much he sacrificed to save us. This is why spending time reading God's Word, times of prayer and fasting, and time spent in contemplation are so valuable. Opening our hearts and minds to Jesus's love for us increases our confidence in his ability to offer us refuge, rescue, and revelatory wisdom.

As an added bonus, an increase in God-confidence equates to greater self-confidence, too, because the truth is that God loves us because we're *us*. How can we not think more highly of ourselves, given what Jesus was willing to sacrifice to be our home? It has taken many years, but I know now that God likes it when I get a little uppity and raise my hand to go in the game. He thinks it's fantastic when I believe my contribution matters. God has never once wanted me to be afraid to share my perspective or offer my talents to the world. Even the most cursory reading of the parable of the talents in Matthew 25 proves that Jesus wants every one of us in the game, offering to do as much as we can with the gifts and talents God gave us.

When Jesus is our home, we can be confident in his power to save and redeem and rescue us, and we can be confident in who we are and what we have to offer. Ultimately, though, one privilege provided to us when we live in Jesus surpasses any other. Eternal life is a tremendous real estate perk, and amazingly, it comes to us without any additional HOA fees.

Our Forever Home

True confession: I go to the gym just to watch HGTV. I mean, it's not like I bring in a sleeve of Girl Scout Cookies and a folding chair to set up in the cardio room. I do walk on the treadmill while watching those home shows. But if the gym canceled its cable subscription, I wouldn't go. This has been proven by the fact that I rarely work out in hotels when there are no televisions available. While this may seem like a weird first-world privilege detail of my life, I will defend my shallow television-inspired self-care by asserting that I'm not picky about which reality home and garden show I watch. Is it a real estate show involving a single woman who is a part-time kindergarten balloon-art teacher looking for a million-dollar condo in Toronto? Wonderful! Is it a home renovation show in which three bathrooms, a kitchen, and an entire basement are renovated in four weeks? Fantastic! Or could it possibly be a cute farmhouse fixer-upper show where a millionaire and his heiress wife buy a working fifty-acre farm in Waco for $150 and turn it into a hotel and amusement park for at-risk puppies? I will cry when they show those puppies playing on the merry-go-round at the end, no doubt about it.

I love houses and homes. I love seeing the kinds of places people want to live. I find the diversity of housing available in the world endlessly intriguing. Witnessing the renovation thrills me.

Hearing a designer say "Welcome home!" to a family sounds like Jesus's best line on repeat again and again.

But truth be told, those shows generally leave me feeling a little disillusioned with my own worldly abode. I don't have the killer view of downtown that the balloon artist enjoys every day. Nor do I have a basement retreat where my teens can entertain one hundred friends on a Friday night. And for sure, I paid more than that couple paid for their farm in Waco, despite living only an hour and a half away.

Home television shows prick my heart for a forever home that will never be less than everything I want and need it to be. Of course, despite what your realtor or contractor may say, forever homes don't exist here on Earth, mainly because living forever here on Earth isn't possible. But that doesn't mean living forever in our forever home isn't available at all. Paul wrote about all this in his second letter to the church in Corinth:

> For we know that if our earthly tent we live in is
> destroyed, we have a building from God, an eternal
> dwelling in the heavens, not made with hands. Indeed,
> we groan in this tent, desiring to put on our heavenly
> dwelling, since, when we are clothed, we will not be
> found naked. Indeed, we groan while we are in this
> tent, burdened as we are, because we do not want to
> be unclothed but clothed, so that mortality may be
> swallowed up by life. Now the one who prepared us for
> this very purpose is God, who gave us the Spirit as a
> down payment.
>
> So we are always confident and know that while we
> are at home in the body we are away from the Lord. For
> we walk by faith, not by sight. In fact, we are confident,
> and we would prefer to be away from the body and at

home with the Lord. Therefore, whether we are at home or away, we make it our aim to be pleasing to him. For we must all appear before the judgment seat of Christ, so that each may be repaid for what he has done in the body, whether good or evil. (2 Cor. 5:1–10 CSB)

These glorified tents we live in, no matter how well-designed or beautiful they are, will all erode and fall down one day. The loss can happen slowly or in a single moment. People who have lost their homes in a fire, an earthquake, a monsoon, or other natural disasters often say they occasionally forget that they've lost certain things. They'll think of a sweater they want to wear or a book they want to read before remembering it was part of the destruction. The memory often begins the mourning all over again. The temporary nature of creation seems cruel at times.

Paul, though, reminds us that we have an eternal dwelling in the heavens, and it can never be destroyed. In fact, Paul asserts that what we lose and mourn in this life isn't life at all, but our mortality. Our true purpose is to see our mortality swallowed up by life in Christ.

Jesus came to consume our earthly homes that could never house us forever so we can live in him for all eternity.

A few days ago, I drove my son downtown to meet a photographer for his senior photos. My son will turn eighteen next week, actually. He is my oldest and the first person whose life I have borne witness to from birth to adulthood. Parenting is a crazy trip to take on any given day, but for the child I once housed in my body and held in my arms to be seven inches taller than I am and a legal adult is nothing short of mind-blowing. We took our trip downtown because photos seemed like a good way to document the miracle of being grown-ish.

We arrived early that day and parked at our favorite taco place. Free parking in downtown Austin is a luxury. But then we realized the restaurant was closed, and the signs warned we might be towed. I'm a worst-case scenario avoider who would rather not have her car impounded, so we searched for another spot. A block away, on South Congress Avenue, we found glorious street parking. All I had to do was back my large SUV, with its broken side mirror, into the spot. I went for it, fully confident in Jesus and my stellar parking skills. My son opened the door to check my placement. "Perfect!" he said. I'm not sure how he could have ever doubted team Mom and Jesus.

I thought about that parking spot later. I thought about how thrilling it is to happen upon the perfect spot downtown. I'm not totally sure why scarcity makes the blessing of a good parking spot seem like a personal validation of my worth as a human. When the right spot comes to me at the right time, the good parking spot seems to prove my own goodness and worthiness. And if it took skill to squeeze my car into that spot, well, I've proven myself even more worthy of the blessing. Faith and works thrive in our ideas about downtown parking, especially when we consider a pristine spot to be linked to some kind of parking version of eternal security. We can never let that good parking spot go, you guys!

But parking spots are pretty much the opposite of a forever home. What's more temporary than a parking spot? When I lived in downtown Los Angeles, I had to park on the street every day. There were weeks when I avoided driving anywhere because I had found such a killer spot. I walked to restaurants. I bummed rides off friends to the grocery store. I had such a great spot! I couldn't give it up! But of course, eventually, I had to give it up to go to work or drive to a friend's house in the Valley. I always felt a little jealous of the driver that pulled up as I pulled out. *Ah yes, the new chosen one has arrived.*

Watching my son take his senior photos while my car sat in its perfect parking spot the other day, I tried not to get too sentimental about him, the one God chose to add to our family first. I have watched good and bad seasons come and go in his life. I thought the sleepless nights of infancy would swallow us all whole. I laughed through so many days of his early childhood; he embodied joy and fun. But he also once lay sick on the bathroom floor as a preteen and asked me why God let people suffer. I held his head and answered honestly, "I don't really know." I can't count how many times I shouted "That's my baby!" as he rounded third base for a home run or threw a touchdown pass. These last few years, as he's faced frustrations on the path to adulthood, I've cried alone in my room a few times because I wanted everything to be different for him, better for him.

But really, in every season of his life, we were just parked temporarily, like we parked on South Congress that morning. Some spots were just better than others.

Every day of our lives, Jesus watches us back into our temporary spots with his arms open wide to us as our true eternal home. We know this is true because God calls us his own kids, bragging about our home runs, sitting on the cold tile floor with us when we're sick, and checking out our best parking jobs, and then saying "Perfect!" with a big thumbs up. First John 3 proves this and even promises that Jesus is heading back for us someday:

> See what great love the Father has given us that we
> should be called God's children—and we are! The
> reason the world does not know us is that it didn't know
> him. Dear friends, we are God's children now, and what
> we will be has not yet been revealed. We know that
> when he appears, we will be like him because we will see
> him as he is. (1 John 3:1–2 CSB)

I have not always been a perfect parent; but no matter how old my kids get, I hope they always feel at home with me. That desire sums up how Jesus loves us. He offers us himself, and his love pulls us into God the Father's forever family home, which is unlike any home we will ever know here on Earth. We are the permanently chosen ones in his love. I hope that sounds like much better news than a good parking spot to you. Even better news is coming in Chapter Four, though. We have a date with the church, and it may or may not be love at first sight.

Part Two

Love
Experiencing Life in Community

Joining God in Relational Communion

CHAPTER 4

Love
and Online Dating

"Guess what? I have flaws. What are they? Oh, I don't know.
I sing in the shower. I spend too much time volunteering.
Sometimes I hit people with my car. So sue me."

—Michael Scott[1]

I was married just before online dating became a viable option for meeting someone interesting. There was not a smartphone to be found at my wedding. Media had not yet gone social. We still read paper newspapers back in 2001. Our wedding photographs were not digital. The Knot was something we tied figuratively, not a website where brides and grooms created a whole online universe regarding the details of their big day. Truth be told, I hadn't even heard of a text the day I said "I do."

---

[1] *The Office*, season 4, episode 1, "Fun Run," aired September 27, 2007, on NBC.

Back then, if you wanted to meet a potential date, you did all the legwork yourself.[2] You put on real clothes to attend a party at a friend's house, where you made (or avoided) eye contact with live human people. You then passed through the sea of small talk to find out where he or she grew up and whether you liked similar music and books, and you attempted to decide if you could stand an entire night of this person's horsey laugh flying in your face from their big mouth.

I was unwilling to do all this, which explains how I ended up falling in love with my oldest friend. He didn't care if I wore sweats to dinner. I was appropriately prepared for a lifetime of his obsession with classic rock and *The Lord of the Rings*. Despite my obnoxious laugh, I wooed him with my quick wit and an exuberant flair for the dramatic. In my experience, a good red lipstick and a wicked sense of humor can ruin a man's ability to be logical quickly, no app required.

However, had online dating apps been more readily available, I probably would have enjoyed scrolling through profiles while eating chips and salsa at an introverted pajama party for one. After asking real-life online daters about the process, however, I've learned that finding a date on an app is not always a shortcut to meeting quality people without being required to socialize. Like everything that happens online, it's complicated.

Generally, the complications arise when people are weird and lie on their profiles. Given the ease with which a person can be Googled these days, I'm not sure how anyone gets away with claiming to have earned imaginary advanced degrees while acting in top-tier Hollywood movies and simultaneously competing as

---

[2] The exception to this rule was, of course, the *You've Got Mail* scenario. Meeting in a chat room and then realizing you are madly in love with a sworn business enemy is a wonderful trope. Also, if you read *Holy Guacamole*, you know how I feel about Tom Hanks movies. #cannotgetenough

an Olympic weightlifter. But go ahead and shoot your shot, my friend. Seems 0.5 percent legit. Other weirdos substitute a photo of a more attractive person for their profile pic. I suppose they just let the chips fall when they meet their date in public, and the revelation hits that she is not, in fact, Jennifer Lopez's twin sister. Live and learn, I guess.

But worst of all are the blessed strangers who can't distinguish the fine line between expressing enthusiastic interest and becoming an online stalker. These stories activate my anticipate-and-prepare-for-the-worst-case-scenario hardwiring, effectively ruining my romanticized introvert idea of online dating. I know now that if Morgan doesn't outlive me, I will never have the guts to utilize the Internet to find another human being who finds me bearable but is not a psychopath.

As I consider the world of online dating, I'm struck by how similar its drama is to church drama. Church can be a wild ride through humanity's oddness, too. I am thankful for the people who love the church and consider it a blissfully wonderful experience no matter how crazy the train ride gets. But some of us swipe left every time the church train enters slightly perilous territory.

Let's take a ride on the church wild side, shall we?

Old-Timey Church

Church hasn't always been like online dating. It hasn't always involved websites that potentially promise one kind of expertise or experience and then fail to deliver. Church hasn't always been glossier and prettier in photos than it is in real life. And most of all, choosing a church hasn't always been so strangely similar to a night spent on a dating app or an episode of *The Bachelor*, where church seekers line up all the possible churches in their city to offer one lucky lady a rose.

In the beginning, there was only one "church" in every city. Just to be clear, the church in each city wasn't a building with a pulpit and a robustly robed choir. Early Christians gathered in homes to worship. But, generally speaking, if you believed Jesus was the Son of God and you lived in Rome, you were a member of the Roman church. If you were a Christian in Philippi, you were bound to love your church, since it was Paul's favorite and had a stellar preacher named Lydia. Should you happen to have been a Christian in ancient Corinth, you would've worshiped with everyone else in the Corinthian church, which was a spirited crew who certainly did not lack enthusiasm for spiritual gifts. Paul's letters to the Corinthians remind us that the church isn't hard to navigate because there are so many different church profiles in our Google search for "best church in my city." The church is hard to navigate for the same reason online dating can be a horror story: it's the people who will make you cringe.[3]

Paul gives us one of those horror stories to kick off his first letter to those Corinthians (good times):

> Now I urge you, brothers and sisters, in the name of
> our Lord Jesus Christ, that all of you agree in what you
> say, that there be no divisions among you, and that you
> be united with the same understanding and the same
> conviction. For it has been reported to me about you,
> my brothers and sisters, by members of Chloe's people,
> that there is rivalry among you. What I am saying is
> this: One of you says, "I belong to Paul," or "I belong
> to Apollos," or "I belong to Cephas," or "I belong to
> Christ." Is Christ divided? Was Paul crucified for you?

---

[3] If you and I have ever attended the same church, I am *clearly* not talking about you here. You and I were probably the only normal, un-cringeworthy people in that church. It was *everyone else* who stacked up dysfunctional behaviors like they were stacking hotcakes at a pancake breakfast fundraiser.

Or were you baptized in Paul's name? I thank God
that I baptized none of you except Crispus and Gaius,
so that no one can say you were baptized in my name.
(1 Cor. 1:10–15 CSB)

Here, Paul was addressing a tear in the church over which
Christians followed which leaders. There was the "Paul party,"
the "Apollos party," and the "Peter party."[4] Different groups of
Corinthian Christians identified with different Christian leaders.
When this scenario plays out today, we hear people say, "Sure, we
go to (fill in the blank) church, but we feel more connected to the
teaching of (fill in the blank), the podcaster/author/preacher I
listen to online." The problem created by this super-fandom craze
in Paul's day (and in our own) wasn't that these Christians were
claiming allegiance to a leader to affirm that leader. The damaging
and dysfunctional part of that situation was that these Christians
were claiming allegiance to certain human leaders to affirm themselves. As in, they really didn't think that Apollos was great; they
thought they were great for following Apollos. We can like all
the podcasters and preachers we want to like, but when we feel
like spiritually elite Christians because we identify with a human
leader, we have lost the plot of Christianity.

Paul claimed then, and I still claim now, that when superfan
cliques arise in our faith communities, it threatens to tear the
church apart. These days, a great deal of this damage is done online.

When you consider the way some Christians treat one
another in the comment section on social media, do Paul's words
somber your heart as much as they do mine? Like Facebook and
Twitter and Instagram, the first church was a place where people
of many different racial, religious, cultural, and socioeconomic

---

[4]Hey, Paul, can I be part of the Holy Ghost party? 'Cause a Holy Ghost party
don't stop!

backgrounds arrived in one place and tried to figure out how to relate to one other in a new kind of space. They tried to figure out how their faith in Christ affected their diets, their romantic and sexual relationships, their finances, and everything else. Conflicts galore resulted from the diversity of experiences and perspectives. But back then, when your pastor started saying things you couldn't relate to/disagreed with/weren't sure about/didn't want to hear about that week, there wasn't a more appealing or less offensive church to flee to.

Early Christians didn't have thousands of years of church history to cling to like a lifesaving flotation device while people without access to their raft sank beneath the waters. Nor did they have thousands of years of church history to throw like gasoline on the bonfire of deconstruction. Early Christians carved out what a diverse community of Christians should look like, based on the eyewitness testimonies of Jesus's disciples, the Jewish scriptures, and their conflicts with one another.

Speaking of conflicts, in Acts 6:1, we read about the Hellenistic Jews and Hebraic Jews in the Jerusalem church duking it out over whose widows were receiving better care. In Galatians 2, Paul spills the tea about his conflict with Peter over Peter's racist practice of separating himself from the Gentile believers. And who can forget the conflict in Acts 5, between Peter and a married couple named Ananias and Sapphira, when Peter rightly accused them of lying and cheating the church, at which point they both dropped dead.[5]

While I doubt Paul thought spontaneous death would continue to plague immature and deceitful Christians, he certainly realized all the conflict and confrontation would wear everybody down. He knew we would need structures to help us create healthy,

---

[5] Talk about a bummer of a meeting!

holy communities, sustained by everyone's unique contribution. But he also knew we would need more than that. We would need "an even better way."

> Now you are the body of Christ, and individual members of it. And God has appointed these in the church: first apostles, second prophets, third teachers, next miracles, then gifts of healing, helping, leading, various kinds of tongues. Are all apostles? Are all prophets? Are all teachers? Do all do miracles? Do all have gifts of healing? Do all speak in tongues? Do all interpret? But desire the greater gifts. And I will show you an even better way. (1 Cor. 12:27–31)

Paul goes on in the Very Famous Passage (more on that to come) in 1 Corinthians 13 to tell us that identifying our purpose, role, and gifting is garbage if we don't love well while we do it. Have you ever taken one of those spiritual gifts tests? I've taken about 473, and I'm still not entirely sure which gifts God has bestowed upon me. (I serve Jesus based on my mood, I guess.)

But the good news/bad news of those tests is, if you can figure out how the questionnaire is going, you can manipulate the answers to best serve yourself. You could proudly score higher than your pastor (good news) but wind up horrified by the possibility you will one day be in charge of the church (bad news).[6] Want to know what 1 Corinthians says is better than being a pastor, a prophet, or an apostle? Being patient and kind with one another. Not being arrogant or rude. In the famous passage of 1 Corinthians 13, Paul offers us what might be the most impossible spiritual laundry list

---

[6]Trust me when I say that being in charge of a church is rarely a picnic—even on the day you have a church picnic. It always rains when our church plans outdoor fun activities, and someone ends up mad, at home, and with too much potato salad in her fridge. (Usually, it's me.)

outside of the Sermon on the Mount: believing the best about one another, rejoicing in the truth, and enduring through whatever comes our way. Love, Paul says, has nothing to do with flexing our best spiritual gift or going to the hottest new church plant in town with the killer viral preacher. However, love can make us superstars in the body of Christ.

Our spiritual gifts are sort of like the towels the generous guests gifted me at my wedding. They will cease to be useful someday. Everyone's influence and leadership will someday pass to the next generation. Our disputes and allegiances are destined to become ancient and mostly forgotten history. All the cultural debates and arguments that arise from our diverse viewpoints and needs will one day end. But "Love never ends," Paul wrote in 1 Corinthians 13:8 (csb).

Love, he says, literally lasts forever.

Maybe this is what he had in mind in Romans 8, where Paul claimed that creation itself groans with labor pains as the gospel births God's children into existence. Another version of this passage says it like this: "All around us we observe a pregnant creation. The difficult times of pain throughout the world are simply birth pangs. But it's not only around us; it's *within* us" (Rom. 8:22–23 *The Message*).

Paul suggested here that the conflicts we experience in life and our churches are the labor pains of love.

Does anyone want to get married and have a church baby?

Church Babies

Because Paul used pregnancy and childbirth as a teaching tool, I suggest we drop anchor for a hot minute and do our best to view church through a baby-birthing lens. This, I think, is far more crucial to do than we may have realized, so here goes.

Just as men and women share a masculine metaphorical inheritance as the sons (and therefore heirs) of God, men and women share a feminine metaphorical identity as the bride of Christ. As Christ's bride, we share the call to give birth through the metaphorical contractions that hit our churches as God births through his Spirit what he has implanted within us.

Let's break down this idea by first recalling how babies are made. You may have learned from your parents (great), learned from friends at school (probably less great), or learned from the Internet (definitely not great) that pregnancy requires the union of diverse bodies and parts. Babies are not the result of homogenous relationships. Babies happen when we get very familiar and extra close with people wholly unlike ourselves.[7]

Consider, then, this idea of diverse union creating life and how it connects to the Christian faith. Christians believe that all of life sprang from the Trinity, which we understand to be three distinct and diverse persons united as one God. Diversity within a loving community, therefore, is of high value to God. When we consider the language Jesus himself used to describe the kind of union he prayed we would have, we see that God has always planned for his people to come together as one in him.

> I pray not only for these, but also for those who believe
> in me through their word. May they all be one, as you,
> Father, are in me and I am in you. May they also be in
> us, so that the world may believe you sent me. I have
> given them the glory you have given me, so that they
> may be one as we are one. I am in them and you are in
> me, so that they may be made completely one, that the

---

[7] In the spirit of the Song of Songs, let's get comfortable with discussions involving both sex and God, shall we?

> world may know you have sent me and have loved them
> as you have loved me. (John 17:20–23 CSB)

Why did Jesus say we need to be completely one? Jesus explained in verse 23 when he said, "so . . . that the world may know [God has] sent me and [has] loved them as [he has] loved me" (John 17:23 CSB).

Just as babies are evidence that a couple has (in theory) deeply loved one another, the diverse and glorious church, where people from so many different nations and races and backgrounds and perspectives love one another deeply, is evidence of God's miraculous and salvific love.

Just as the initial "contact" required to make human babies can be exceedingly enjoyable, the beginning of a spiritual relationship with someone very different than ourselves is often super fun. How interesting they are! We get caught up in the glory of having a church baby with quirky, unusual, strange-to-us, new Christian friends. We are thrilled at the prospect of creating a whole new life together as a community of faith. Just like with babies, the cost and sacrifice are not always considered when we decide to make that church baby.

But if you've ever been pregnant or have been in any church for any amount of time, you know the sacrifice and pain involved in the labor catch up with you eventually. You will, no doubt, believe me when I tell you that, over the years, we have had hundreds and hundreds of people come to our politically, socioeconomically, and racially diverse church, thrilled with the prospect of entering a community where they are surrounded by people unlike themselves. These people sincerely become caught up in the miracle of a spiritual family that is led by a diverse team of women and men who are passionate about reaching our city with the love of Christ.

They often say something like "this is what heaven will look like," and they aren't wrong.

I hope you will also believe me when I report that when an election or a police shooting or, say, the odd pandemic comes along, the very same people who swore "this is what heaven looks like" can't believe that any Christian could actually do/believe/say "that." And by "that," I mean any cultural perspective different from their own. If you've had a physical baby, you know that biological labor is painful. When there is disagreement and conflict over how to handle crises and cultural upheaval, church labor is equally painful. At some point we all look up and tell our Great Physician, "I'd like that epidural, please and thank you."

Birthing is painful, but I've come to learn that the pain only highlights the miracle.

What else was Paul after when he pointed to the pain as evidence that love lasts and is doing way more than we could have hoped for? The miracle is *us*. The body of Christ is one big old beautiful church baby. And the rest of Romans 8 reads kind of like a nurse's baby checklist. As you read Paul's words, you can hear a nurse telling a new mother, *Your baby has a squishy nose, a weird thing that will fall off and become just a regular belly button, lips that can suck until your skin bruises, and the best roly-poly feet ever that can also fit in the baby's mouth* (which is weird but super cool). Nurse Paul's list of the attributes of those who have been born of God's Spirit into God's family is less cute but just as helpful. What makes a gloriously cute church baby, Paul?

- In Romans 8:27, Paul says the Spirit of God intercedes for us, praying the will of God in our lives.
- In Romans 8:28–29, we are told that God weaves everything that happens to us into something good and redemptive so we can become more like our Father.

- In Romans 8:31, we read that nothing can ever separate any of us from God's love.
- In Romans 8, we find the most hope we can muster for our church baby to grow and mature and become the bride of Christ in all her glory.

No, in all these things we are more than conquerors through him who loved us. For I am persuaded that neither death nor life, nor angels nor rulers, nor things present nor things to come, nor powers, nor height nor depth, nor any other created thing will be able to separate us from the love of God that is in Christ Jesus our Lord. (Rom. 8:37–39 CSB)

Paul said we don't need to be conquerors who win all the debates and who are always right about every issue. We don't need to find the perfect pastor who can preach and love and kill it on social media. We don't need to elect the perfect ruler in our nation or summon angels with our prayers. God's will is not dependent on us attaining the highest places of authority.

Paul insisted again that love is what we need most; love lasts forever.

Those conflicts (aka contractions) in church are vital to the birthing process. We might think we want a conflict-free church, but every pregnant woman knows that before a baby can be born, you need to feel some pain.

When I was pregnant with my first baby, I decided toward the end of the pregnancy to try to hurry the process along and do something to make the contractions start. I wanted it to be over already. Someone suggested exercise might help. So I went over to a friend's house and climbed up and down her stairs for almost an hour. Then I returned home and waited for my water to break.

My water did not break. However, I felt close to death once I lay on my sofa and attempted to summon contractions with my mind powers. Every part of my body screamed with pain except my uterus. Sometimes you make choices in life and end up stuck with them. Walking up and down stairs while pregnant can be like that, as can hiking, now that I think about it.

A Tale of Two Mountains

My husband and several of his pastor friends take a yearly trip to Colorado to pray and encourage one another. They go fly-fishing and whitewater rafting and then return home refreshed and ready to birth God's church babies. A few years ago, he came home with a story I was not prepared to hear, and it both terrified me and sent me doubled over, laughing at these ridiculous men I love so much.

It was summer, so they decided to take a gondola up the mountain to hike some of the more remote trails. Morgan and his friend Dan took the lead in this excursion, following the poorly marked trail as best as they could. The hike should have taken a couple of hours, but two hours in, they were lost, miles away from the trailhead. One friend began to suffer from altitude sickness and could barely walk. My husband is an outdoorsy person who generally doesn't feel nervous about anything in the wilderness. But after three hours of hiking without any recognizable trail markers, Morgan began to feel a little anxious.

Then they came upon a sign with a skull and crossbones on it that read, "WARNING: You are leaving the ski resort. YOU CAN DIE. This is your decision point." After reading these words, Morgan's friend James somehow found a cellular signal ten thousand feet up that mountain and called his wife, Debbie. Morgan, pretending to look at the map, stood near enough to James to eavesdrop. "Baby, if Morgan and Dan get us more lost and we don't make it back to the gondola before it shuts down, I want you to know that I love you. Tell the boys . . . tell the boys . . . I love them, too," he whispered into the phone.

The hike was getting real.

Morgan and Dan consulted the map with increased focus at this point. They poked around a little, looked for markers, finally figured out where they were, and gave everyone an update. Since the gondola was the only way over impassable rock formations, there was only one hope, really. Morgan broke the news to everyone.

"The good news is that we know where we are. The bad news is that we're an hour and a half from the gondola, and it closes in an hour. We need to move fast, or we won't be able to get back to our hotel tonight."

Just then, because God thought he would up the stress and pressure on these five friends whose lives and relationships hung in the balance, rain began to fall.

These men had chosen to take a hike. There was no undoing or abandoning that choice once the hike took an unexpected turn. The sign that warned they were at a decision point was correct. Theoretically, they could have abandoned one another or decided to just live on the mountain forever. But those were not real options. They pressed on and made it to the gondola long after closing time, hoping for a miracle. And they got one. Debbie must have prayed a powerful prayer because some ritzy private party down in the village had paid to keep it open for the night so people could go up and come down as they pleased. Morgan and all his friends rode down in relative silence and eternal relief. They enjoyed a slightly tense dinner together. The conflict and pain on the mountain stretched their love for one another, and they all laugh about that hike now.

Jesus took Peter, James, and John on a hike in Matthew 17. They didn't have a gondola, nor did they get lost. Peter wasn't calling his wife to tell her he loved her when he suggested they camp there on the mountain because Moses and Elijah, long dead, suddenly appeared on the mountain as Jesus was transfigured into his heavenly glory.

God the Father had words for exuberant Peter. In Matthew 17:5 (CSB), his voice rang out from heaven, "This is my beloved Son, with whom I am well-pleased. Listen to him!" Then Peter, James, and John fell on their faces, terrified.

I always imagine the Mount of Transfiguration like the last night of a supremely awesome youth camp with a light show blazing and smoke machine pumping as a super cool rapper gives his testimony about how growing up in church is hard but loving Jesus is easy. The kids are always crying all over each other and praying for one another, and most of them think that if they could just stay right there forever, life would be immensely better. If everyday life could be like camp, they might be able to handle the peer pressure they face at school. They would stop using a tiny blade to open up the skin on the inside of their thigh. They would be less insecure about sharing their faith. They wouldn't be afraid of failing or disappointing their coaches, parents, friends, or teachers if they stayed at the last night of camp forever.

Many of us wish our church life could be like the last night of camp. Like Peter, we'd like to stay in the places where Jesus is so clearly radiant and well-connected. If we could just find a group of people who seem divinely holy, we would love to camp out on the holiest mountain with just the five of us enjoying our exclusive access to God.

Because I am human and have therefore wrestled with my own sins of entitlement and jealousy, I do wonder if Peter didn't assume that he, James, and John had hit the relational jackpot by being invited up the mountain. James and John probably thought something similar. After all, they were the brothers who approached

Jesus with their mother and applied for a promotion to the highest VIP disciple status later in Matthew 20. God's resonating voice, commanding them to listen to Jesus, was terrifying because it made it clear that none of the glorious last-night-at-camp vibes had anything to do with them.

Sadly, however, the mountaintop high was not their inheritance any more than a perfectly happy church life is ours. Sometimes, our moment on the mountain is a brief gift to witness God's greatness and listen to his beloved Son.

We don't know why Jesus invited only three of the disciples on that hike, leaving the rest of the disciples at the bottom of the mountain with the multitude of people following Jesus. If Peter, James, and John felt special for being invited up the mountain, the thrill dissipated quickly when they arrived back with the other disciples and the multitudes of church babies.

A man with a son who was suffering from seizures had asked for his son to be healed. When the uninvited-to-the-hike disciples were unable to heal the boy, Jesus reacted with strong words:

> "You unbelieving and perverse generation, how long
> will I be with you? How long must I put up with you?
> Bring him here to me." Then Jesus rebuked the demon,
> and it came out of him, and from that moment the boy
> was healed.
>
> Then the disciples approached Jesus privately and
> said, "Why couldn't we drive it out?"
>
> "Because of your little faith," he told them. "For truly
> I tell you, if you have faith the size of a mustard seed,
> you will tell this mountain, 'Move from here to there,'
> and it will move. Nothing will be impossible for you."
> (Matt. 17:17–20 CSB)

Jesus came down what seemed like an impossibly holy mountain and proceeded to tell everyone about a second mountain they could command to move with the tiniest speck of faith. He was fed up with their lack of faith.

Just as Peter, James, and John probably felt like the elite squad and Jesus's premier disciples, the disciples Jesus left behind probably felt a little offended that they didn't score an invite. Their failure to heal the boy may have confirmed their worst fears: that they were not the kind of people God chose to use. Of course, *none* of us have ever felt this way when our peers have been promoted to places of greater influence or access to power. We don't know *anything* about linking our worth and value with our ability to meet the needs of the people in our lives. Not us. Nope. No way. (Yes way.)

What is really happening here in Matthew 17?

Jesus showed us two mountains. On one, we behold the glory of God and the way we have been invited into a mystical relational connection with the triune God and all the saints before us. On the other, we behold the messy and problematic nursery of humanity. That second mountain involved people and their lack of faith to heal their community.

Jesus said it doesn't matter if you're exalted high atop a majestic mountain or feel rejected at the bottom of a messy one. Your position doesn't matter when you have faith for the miraculous.

And lest we forget our Bible stories, Moses and Elijah were no strangers to mountainous conflict and drama. Moses and Elijah had their own hike-up-a-mountain-with-God stories. In Numbers 11, Moses took the worst hiking excursion ever, with the members of his church complaining until Moses kind of freaked out on God.

In 1 Kings 18 and 19, Elijah saw God move miraculously when he confronted Ahab and the prophets of Baal on Mount Carmel.

But his fear of Ahab and Jezebel, combined with the people's lack of permanent repentance, sent him into a deep depression.

I wonder if, while on the Mount of Transfiguration, Moses, Elijah, and Jesus discussed how God's answer to the problems in Numbers 11 and 1 Kings 19 involved a kind of communal care and leadership. God had instructed Moses to gather seventy men to help Moses lead. In 1 Kings 19, God told Elijah which leaders he needed to appoint to help him.

It takes two people to make a baby and one woman to do the birthing. But it takes a whole community to raise and shape a child into a person of integrity and faith.

Do we have the faith to speak to the mountain called church and see God move? Can we see that Jesus's frustration with the disciples in Matthew 17 reveals what Paul claimed throughout his descriptions of the church (namely, that God's plan for meeting the needs of a community involves everyone in the community working together)?

I want to imagine Matthew 17 ending a different way. I want to imagine Jesus, Peter, James, and John coming down the mountain and Andrew running up to Peter, telling the incredible story about how Thomas cast that demon out of the little boy. And then I want the boy's parents to say they were so inspired that they prayed for five more people after their son was healed, and all of them were healed too. I want Matthew to get worked up as he describes how revival broke out, the multitude began praying for one another, and miracles were happening left and right. Peter would be jealous he missed the action, of course. John would begin laughing with joy.

Who would ever swipe left on a community that loves and cares for them like that? On bad days, it seems impossible we could ever live up to this imagined profile pic of the church. Do we need a new podcast or a fresh spiritual practice to pull it off? Is there a supplement we can take or some oil we can diffuse to turn us into that kind of mature, loving community?

Amazingly, no.

God's plan to mature us so we can thrive as the body of Christ is good and it is messy. It proves sometimes things must get worse before they can get better.

And things, well, they're about to get really messy around here.

Love
as an Old Truck

"I've had a good run. I've built a lot of things that work
and a lot of things that don't work."

—Carroll Shelby

I drive a white 2001 Toyota Sequoia we named Old Bessie.[1]

Bessie is not exactly in tippity-top shape. She would never win a car beauty pageant. If you convinced me to race for pinks, you would certainly win the race; but taking Bessie home might wind up a sum-all loss for you. Sometimes I dream of the day I walk outside and find a shiny new vehicle in my driveway. Until then, her many dings and dents tell the thrilling tales that Bessie and I have lived through together.

---

[1] This fact is either proof that authors really don't make any money or that I have decided to keep the old beast until it becomes a "classic" so I can be cool like that. (Welcome to my TED Talk on how to spin a sad reality into a romantic tale of awesomeness.)

Bessie's right side mirror droops uselessly toward the ground because I clipped a parked truck's side mirror on my way home after school drop-off one day.[2] The mini accident was pure suburban drama, ending with a bathrobed man threatening to use his video surveillance footage to prove I was responsible for the accident. This surprised me since I had knocked on his door to offer to pay to fix his car. *No video necessary, sir. I'm standing right here.*

On another occasion, I backed Bessie's rear bumper into an invisible cement pole in a Nordstrom parking garage. Because the pole was not there when I looked in my rearview mirror, I assume a Hogwarts student and a massive invisibility cloak were involved.

Last May, I scraped Bessie's rear bumper along a metal building with a parking lot the size of a postage stamp. Bessie's limited turning radius played a leading role in that episode of *Carrie Breaks Her Car.*

However, although I am her primary caregiver, I am not the sole abuser of Old Bessie. The passengers I haul to baseball practices, ballet rehearsals, and school events have increased Bessie's shabby chicness over the years. My kids have left paper cups of soda in cup holders long enough for the cup to disintegrate and leak. The wrappers and stray french fries embedded in her upholstery date as far back as 2016. Flecks of automobile paint have been transformed into confetti when my kids have opened the doors too hard and smacked into trees, walls, and (Jesus be my helper) other cars.

Of course, some of Bessie's weaknesses are simply part of her disintegrating design. If you're expecting 2021 model attributes, Bessie is bound to disappoint you. Her antenna is broken, and her radio is useless. Her retro-cool cassette tape deck is nonfunctional. Her rear door latch breaks about once every three years (this is

[2] You can call me Thelma, and I'll call you Louise.

no exaggeration; we've had it repeatedly replaced). Bessie has no working speakers near the backseat, and the passenger-seat speakers have no bass at all. Twenty years of Texas mega-summers have left her leather interior cracked and uncomfortable to sit on. The coup de grâce, however, is Bessie's Very Special Sunroof. If you drive over sixty miles per hour on the highway, Bessie's sunroof will shake and emit a deafening rattling sound. Imagine a jackhammer on the roof of your car, and you have an approximate idea of the noise level.

Does Bessie qualify as a jalopy? Probably.

For the last few years, I have told her, "Bessie, greener pastures are up ahead next year. You're going to love retirement, my friend." But then our circumstances make it clear that a new car is not in the budget. The poor old girl is then forced to make do with our granola-bar-wrapper-littered pastures.

Bessie doesn't mind, though, because she's never really been babied in this world. We are Bessie's second owners. You've heard of the famed car that belonged to the little old lady from Pasadena? Well, Bessie once belonged to a quintessential Texas grandmother: stout body, curly white hair, takes no crap from anyone. Come to think of it, that's a great description of Bessie herself. She is sturdy, despite some general rickety parts. She's got a little fluff and flair to her, including her (broken and rattling) sunroof and (dried out and cracked) leather seats. Like Granny, she does not care what you think of her or how you treat her; she just keeps on truckin'.

What does an old SUV have to do with church, though?

So glad you asked.

A Little Body Work

Bessie serves us beautifully as a working analogy for the church. Like Bessie, the church is sturdy and full of eccentricities and flaws. Both are big and have space for everyone to sit, but neither is the most comfortable place to be. The "drivers" in the church caused some of the cracks and scrapes and brokenness over the years. Immature and careless "passengers" caused others. The church is not just old; she's ancient. Some parts of her get quite noisy when we try to increase our speed to keep up with the flow of traffic. When we try to switch out old parts and ideas for new ones, the changes cause a great deal of debate and expense.

The real kicker is that, just as I often assume we may not need Bessie much longer, a lot of people seem to think the church may not be necessary either.

All around us, people are reexamining their faith and their relationship with the church. According to a 2021 article from Gallup[3] in 1937, over 70 percent of Americans belonged to a church, synagogue, or mosque. However, in a poll conducted by Gallup in 2020, only 47 percent of Americans belonged to one. When the data is broken down generationally, it's clear that the younger an American is, the less likely they are to be a member of a community of faith, and the more likely they are not to identify with any religion whatsoever.

Joining and attending a church on Sundays is no longer a cultural value in the United States. My parents, aunts, and uncles all lament this change. They remember a kind of Sunday I never experienced, when everyone they knew got dressed up, attended church, and then came home to a big Sunday dinner. Stores and businesses closed every Sunday when they were young.

"Life was so good that way!" one of my aunts insisted at dinner a month ago.[4]

---

[3] "U.S. Church Membership Falls Below Majority for First Time," *Gallup*, March 29, 2021, https://news.gallup.com/poll/341963/church-membership-falls-below-majority-first-time.aspx.

[4] She also laments the way cashiers give change back. She wants it counted back to her, change first and then bills. I told her that skill has been lost because almost no one uses cash. "I know! They want me to pay with an *app*. I. Will. Not!" #iloveher

And for her, as a middle-class White woman in the South, life was really good back then.

But for many people, life was not better fifty years ago, despite church attendance being the norm on Sundays. President Lyndon B. Johnson signed the Civil Rights Act in 1964 to end segregation, but racial justice and equality could not be signed into people's hearts. Almost sixty years later, the United States is still working toward redemption and reconciliation in racial justice. Before the Equal Credit Opportunity Act of 1974, banks would only issue a married woman a credit card in her husband's name, and unmarried women were not eligible for credit at all. We've come a long way, baby, but in 2020, women still earned only 84 percent of what men earned in the United States.[5]

While change can often be uncomfortable and unsettling, change that elevates the oppressed and heals our communities is a blessing. Like my aunt, I wish allegiance to God and his people was a higher cultural value for us all. But I wonder if God will use the cultural upheaval and spiritual reexamination happening all around us to create churches where people pursue spiritual growth and a deeper understanding of God instead of settling for a lifeless religious routine. Could relinquishing attending church as only an obligatory act open our hands to a more authentic allegiance to the gospel and a more meaningful engagement in a church community?

I hope so.

Belonging to and regularly attending a church only to fulfill your sense of duty will not worsen your quality of life. However, if fulfilling Christ's call to love God first and others more than yourself is what motivates your steadfast participation and loyalty to your local church, you're eyebrow-deep in a stellar spiritual life.

---

[5] "Gender pay gap in U.S. held steady in 2020," Pew Research Center, May 25, 2021, https://www.pewresearch.org/fact-tank/2021/05/25/gender-pay-gap-facts/.

I know we already drank tea with our friend Paul and listened to his tales of factions and divisions within the church, but I want to revisit the church in Corinth because there's still so much drama to unpack from their story. Not only did the Corinthian church argue about which leader was the best leader to follow, but they also couldn't agree on topics like sexual ethics, marriage, how to handle spiritual practices such as prayer and Communion, how people with authority ought to handle their power and influence, what to do about women speaking in church, and whose spiritual gifts were most boss. Go ahead and read that list again so you can marvel at how church back then wasn't much different than church now.[6]

I'm eternally grateful for Paul's letter to Corinth when Christian community is challenging because it proves that following Jesus has never been easy. Church has never been easy.[7] From the very beginning, churches have dealt with conflict, confusion, elitism, and heresy. Even so, somehow, we're still supposed to be in it all together. Paul broke down that togetherness like this:

> For just as the body is one and has many parts, and all
> the parts of that body, though many, are one body—so
> also is Christ. For we were all baptized by one Spirit into
> one body—whether Jews or Greeks, whether slaves or
> free—and we were all given one Spirit to drink. Indeed,
> the body is not one part but many. If the foot should say,
> "Because I'm not a hand, I don't belong to the body," it is
> not for that reason any less a part of the body. And if the
> ear should say, "Because I'm not an eye, I don't belong to

---

[6] Church history is like the history of every family gathering you've experienced. Everyone in every generation pretty much ends up mad about the same stuff.

[7] Serving Jesus in a time that includes air conditioning and espresso is my preference; the caffeine and cool air help me cope with all the theological and cultural debates.

the body," it is not for that reason any less a part of the body. If the whole body were an eye, where would the hearing be? If the whole body were an ear, where would the sense of smell be? But as it is, God has arranged each one of the parts in the body just as he wanted. (1 Cor. 12:12–18 CSB)

Wouldn't it be strange if your foot decided one day it didn't believe it needed the rest of the body any longer? How much stranger would it be if your foot declared it was no longer part of the body? "Um, body? Hello up there! I'm out. Listen, I can't even any more with the creaky knees and arthritic hands. And that face? Don't get me started. One word: tweezers!" Could your foot survive if it removed itself from other parts of the body that keep the lifeblood flowing to it? Of course not.

A cut-off foot would die and then, you know, rot. Cheery image, no?

But amputation not only causes problems for the body part that is removed; it impacts the body at large as well. What happens to the rest of the body when the foot refuses to engage in the part God created it to play? How can the body go where it needs to go without a foot to take it? It just limps along.

This analogy is extreme and a little gross. But it also whistles at us, clear as a bell, about what's at stake when a Christian becomes cut off from the body of Christ. The first rule of the church is that we don't get to choose to be in the church. The second rule is that God chooses where to put people in the church. The question we must face is, are we faithfully responding to God's chosen arrangement? Are we honoring the call to love and serve his body? Are we submitted to one another in love, placing the needs of others above our own? Do we respect and pray for the leaders God has appointed in our churches? Do we treat others in ways that esteem and nurture them toward a greater knowledge of God?

Dear readers, if you're thinking you'd rather not have to rely on the messed-up churches you've experienced over the years for your eternal spiritual life's blood flow, I don't blame you. After all, authority figures in the church have wounded many of us. How many times has this body of ours been diagnosed with cancerous growths? How many times has the church needed open heart surgery to reconstruct her at the very center? We are not the first generation of believers to deconstruct their faith and reach for a fresh understanding of how to love God and live in community. Relying on the church to function properly and provide life to our weary selves is akin to me relying on Bessie to get us from Texas to Canada on one tank of gas. It seems neither rational nor prudent.

And yet, Ephesians 5:25–27 (CSB) says, "Christ loved the church and gave himself for her to make her holy, cleansing her with the washing of water by the word. He did this to present the church to himself in splendor, without spot or wrinkle or anything like that, but holy and blameless." If we find we can't love the church as Jesus did and wash her with words of prayer and hope and faith and wisdom, perhaps we aren't grasping what's at stake.

WWJDT: Why Would Jesus Do That?

Jesus chose a big, clunky, ancient, uncomfortable, messy community full of people (who do dumb things like drive their cars into cement poles and metal buildings) as his bride. There are nights I lie in bed sleepless because this seems like a terrible strategy. How could a wise God think a broken people could accomplish anything valuable in the world? How could Jesus look at humanity, in all its Bessie glory, and see any possibility for redemption?

I don't think Jesus ever pushed all his chips into the center, betting on just us, flying solo. When he saw our brokenness, he knew we were positively doomed. Jesus's confidence about the fate of the church isn't inspired by our ability to self-crank and manifest a divinely perfect community. Instead, God's confidence in the church's ability to become his bride without a flaw originates in the power of the gospel to continually reform and redeem God's people.

God's intimate investment in the health of the church helps me feel less rankled with the idea of belonging to his messy Bessie. However, my annoyance with all the bad drivers in our churches who can't find a turn signal has not disappeared yet. Fortunately, as we continue in 1 Corinthians 12, Paul's words help me move past my irritation:

> And if they were all the same part, where would the body be? As it is, there are many parts, but one body. The eye cannot say to the hand, "I don't need you!" Or again, the head can't say to the feet, "I don't need you!" On the contrary, those parts of the body that are weaker are indispensable. And those parts of the body that we consider less honorable, we clothe these with greater honor, and our unrespectable parts are treated with greater respect, which our respectable parts do not need.
>
> Instead, God has put the body together, giving greater honor to the less honorable, so that there would be no division in the body, but that the members would have the same concern for each other. So if one member suffers, all the members suffer with it; if one member is honored, all the members rejoice with it.
> (1 Cor. 12:19–26 CSB)

Given the comment section on Facebook, the brash cruelty in so many DMs these days, and the kinds of emails pastors receive from people who claim Jesus as their Lord, it's clear we struggle to live this passage from 1 Corinthians 12. Too often, we create divisions where divisions shouldn't exist, and we choose not to concern ourselves with people whose ideas perplex us or whose needs evade our ability to empathize.

O beautiful, gifted, necessary fellow body parts in this big old body of Christ, the question that surfaces when we face our shared corporate weaknesses and inconsistencies is this: How can we do better? It's one thing to pass the plate to our nameless neighbor on the matter; it's another to own our complicity and show up ready to drive better, to function better, to be a better body part. How can we be the church in a way that honors God?

Paul could feel that money question rising as he wrote his letter to the Corinthians. He begins by pointing out that everyone has different gifts. This letter is sort of Paul's YMCA end-of-season ceremony moment. Whistle around neck, coaching pants pulled up high above his waist, Paul is slapping his clipboard and shouting with great enthusiasm. *Everyone is special! Everyone gets a trophy! Everyone participates! Everyone has a gift!*

Go ahead and laugh, but it's true. Paul did this, in part, because elitism and pride impede people's ability to flourish in true gospel community. As an antidote for elitism and pride, Paul offered them (and us) what I will call humanity OS 2.0 for church members:

> If I speak human or angelic tongues but do not have love, I am a noisy gong or a clanging cymbal. If I have the gift of prophecy and understand all mysteries and all knowledge, and if I have all faith so that I can move mountains but do not have love, I am nothing. And if I give away all my possessions, and if I give over my body in order to boast but do not have love, I gain nothing. (1 Cor. 13:1–3 csb)

Coach Paul wanted us to know that we must love the game and love our team. Without that love, all we do is make a lot of noise and end up with nothing to show for our hard work. We wind up with ball hogs. Fights break out. Elbows meet faces. Flagrant fouls are called. No one wins.

Since Paul was the "king of plain,"[8] he went on to tell us exactly what communal Christian love for one another should look like in the Very Famous Passage from 1 Corinthians 13.[9] According to Paul, the love we offer and receive in Christian community should be like a mom kissing a scraped knee after a bicycle fall: patient and kind. It should not be like me after binging on the *Magnolia* magazine winter issue: envious, boastful, rude, self-seeking, and irritable. Paul even claimed that if repentance has occurred, the church should not be a place where we return again and again to offenses, endlessly rehashing that time the greeter did not smile when we arrived. However, Paul reminded us that rejoicing in the truth and being in the church go together like peas and carrots. Love is tough and resilient, Paul insisted in 1 Corinthians 13:7. It holds up through the worst storms, it can't be beaten or battered into defeat, and it even stands securely under extreme scrutiny.

It seems impossible for every church in the world to pull this off. Perhaps the foot has cut itself off too many times. Perhaps the arm has slapped the ear too often. And maybe all the parts should pay more attention to the nose.

I only bring this last part up because it, ahem, sometimes kind of stinks in church.

---

[8] All apologies to Sting and The Police.

[9] Please note, 1 Corinthians 13 is often quoted at weddings, but this passage is not primarily about romantic or marital love. This is vital for us to remember because our culture is perfectly fine with married people loving each other sacrificially, but in many ways, our culture has lost this value in our greater communities.

The Smell of Community

Smells deserve our attention. They're like tiny arrows pointing out important details to our brains. Good and bad odors alike are God's original SEO analytics, attempting to bring the most helpful and important information to our brain's newsfeed. For example, the unique smell of teenagers who have forgotten their deodorant as they journey toward adulthood is how our brains remember to be good parents and teach these humans that proper hygiene is the gift that keeps on giving. In contrast, the smell of perfectly baked bread is a neon arrow in our conscious minds to run to the source of the delicious odor. Go ahead and knead some now if you've gone full-on *Great British Baking Show* while you read. I'll wait.

I didn't realize until well into adulthood that the aromas of my childhood included eucalyptus trees and sour cream and onion potato chips. Every time I open a bag of chips or walk by a friend's diffuser[10] as it puffs out eucalyptus oil mist, I am seven years old, sitting on my parents' brick patio, whiling away a quiet Sunday afternoon.

I've come to trust the ability of my nose to connect what I'm experiencing today with deeper memories and truths. Just as we can smell things in the physical, there is a way to smell things in our hearts and souls as well. Whether we call it the gift of discernment, intuition, empathy, prophetic ability, or just the straight-up superpower of wisdom, we all have some level of ability to sense and smell what cannot be seen or touched. Like when we walk past an airport Auntie Anne's or Cinnabon, the "nose" inside us just starts shouting to get our attention. Despite our lack of hunger, our flimsy willpower melts over hot pretzels and sugar. But discipline is a chat for another day. Today, we're just talking about what the

---

[10] My homeopathic friends are a lifeline for me, and hopefully, between their guidance and the Holy Spirit's intervention, I will avoid accidentally dousing myself with DDT in the form of a new body spray I found on Instagram.

nose knows. And sure enough, a good cinnamon roll has never disappointed my nose.

But I didn't always trust that inner nose as I do now. When I moved to Austin to marry Morgan over twenty years ago, I sniffed out something rotten at the church where we served as university campus ministers. I tried to explain the odor to Morgan one night.

"People shouldn't fear their pastor," I told him. "Respect, yes, but fear? Uh-uh. We shouldn't secretly call the hallway to his office 'The Green Mile.'[11] And our friends shouldn't need to check on us to see if we're okay after being belittled and mocked and humiliated in staff meetings."

I would like to take a little pause here and say that if I could go back in time and change something in my life, it would be our decision not to speak up about this. There are no guarantees that anyone would have listened to us, of course. Part of the reason so many people put up with the abuse being doled out in that church culture at the time was that the scope of the ministry happening around us was awe-inspiring.

People were coming to Christ in droves. The seats at our Sunday services held business leaders, professional athletes, and talented young people with dreams to change the world. We watched broken and fragile marriages become strong and full of love. We prayed for the sick, and they were legitimately and miraculously healed. At our outreaches on the University of Texas campus, hundreds of students repented and were baptized. Despite the strange odor in the office Monday through Friday, those years felt like leaping from one amazing God moment to another.

---

[11] *The Green Mile* is a fictional book/movie by Stephen King, and the phrase refers to the last stretch of green concrete a prisoner walked on his way to be executed. I'm sure you can imagine how this moniker for the hallway didn't deepen feelings of safety and peace while approaching our boss's office.

So we ignored the bad smell. We were the lowest people in the chain of authority; what did we know about how a pastor should relate to his staff? Who were we to ask questions of the gifted, experienced leaders above us?

Morgan and I put our heads down and worked long hours trying to love, lead, and inspire college students to grow in God. We prayed and trusted God with our jobs, our lives, and the future of the church we loved. Morgan swam through staff meetings like he was surrounded by sharks while wearing a suit made of dead fish. I accepted that I would be criticized and rebuked if my words, clothing, ideas, and choices didn't line up with what was considered acceptable for staff wives.

Ministry life back then was awful and lonely at times. Morgan and I felt on the outside of the inner circle time and time again. When he was called a bad leader because our campus Bible studies didn't have thousands of students attending, we were humbled in good and bad ways. While I regret not speaking up about the spiritual abuse being doled out, I don't regret our decision to obey Jesus's command to love and bless those who harm us. Many nights, Morgan and I held hands and asked God for rescue, and then we asked God to bless our pastor financially, spiritually, and relationally as we ignored the lingering stench. Love bears and believes and never gives up, after all.

After a few years of that life, we discovered that my nose was accurate. The exposure of all the moral, financial, ethical, and spiritual lines that had been crossed revealed spiritually wounded people bleeding out all around us. Many of our friends' and coworkers' lives, relationships, and finances were left in shattered pieces.

For us and everyone we loved in our church, our church's minor judgment day came like a thief in the night. One day, my top priority was to make our (scary) pastor the first person we told about our first pregnancy to avoid his wrath. The next day, he was "on sabbatical" because they were investigating his bank account and relationships.

In 1 Thessalonians, Paul writes about remaining alert for God's judgment day. While Paul specifically means the return of Christ, minor judgment days fill our day-to-day lives.

> But you, brothers and sisters, are not in the dark, for this day to surprise you like a thief. For you are all children of light and children of the day. We do not belong to the night or the darkness. So then, let us not sleep, like the rest, but let us stay awake and be self-controlled. For those who sleep, sleep at night, and those who get drunk, get drunk at night. But since we belong to the day, let us be self-controlled and put on the armor of faith and love, and a helmet of the hope of salvation. (1 Thess. 5:4–8 CSB)

Stay awake, Paul cautions us. Stay awake and self-controlled as you encourage one another and watch for judgment day with your armor on. We do the opposite of this too often. We escape the terror of life by putting ourselves into a deep sleep with some form of self-medication. We work too much, drink too much, eat too much, buy too much, or argue and debate too much to let the good smell of the bread of life lead us to what our souls need most of all.

As we walked through that painful season of facing the source of the awful smell in our church, I grieved our decision to ignore the odor for so long. But even more, I grieved the choice our former pastor made to leave the church permanently after we learned the details of his abuse of his authority. He had taught often about what it meant to be a spiritual family. I had believed his words about God bringing us together to reach our city with God's love. It would have been messy and hard if he had stayed, but wouldn't it have been beautiful as well? Some may say our community couldn't have healed with him in the room. But I disagree.

The Ties That Bind Us

In John 8, a group of religious leaders brought a woman who had been caught in adultery to Jesus. The Bible says they were using the woman to try to get Jesus in trouble. The men casually mentioned the command Moses had given to stone adulterers and wanted to know what Jesus thought they should do with her. Jesus wrote some words in the dirt and then suggested that the first stone should be thrown by the person there who had not sinned. Then Jesus wrote some more stuff in the dirt, and all the men left, one by one.

Some people wonder if Jesus spelled out those men's sins there in the dirt. Or perhaps he wrote the names of the women the men had committed adultery with. He could have simply written out the Ten Commandments to remind them of their faults and failures. Whatever Jesus wrote, the words bound the men up with the woman so that none of them were willing to claim they were any freer of sin than she.

What is eternally interesting to me is that Jesus didn't turn to the woman and speak with her until all the men had left.

> When Jesus stood up, he said to her, "Woman, where are they? Has no one condemned you?"
>
> "No one, Lord," she answered.
>
> "Neither do I condemn you," said Jesus. "Go, and from now on do not sin anymore." (John 8:10–11 csb)

Let's talk about the things Jesus didn't do in this passage. Jesus didn't tell her she could no longer remain in the community. He didn't forbid her from associating with the men or women in her town. He didn't worry that her friends or sisters or the girls she walked to the well with every day would fall into some similar sin if she suffered no consequences for her actions. Jesus didn't mark her in some way or lecture her. He didn't suggest she make a clean start somewhere else, where no one would know what she had done. Jesus just told her to go back to her life and not to sin anymore.

When presented with a person accused of immorality and sin by the leaders of the religious community, Jesus did not choose sides. He communicated that everyone deserved judgment and punishment for their sins. We're all connected parts of one body, and flinging rocks at individual people, other local churches, or at the church as a whole because sin has been discovered is not just a bad idea. It's bad theology.

For Morgan and me, that stinky church never stopped feeling like the place we were supposed to be. Morgan was offered other ministry positions elsewhere during our years there. It probably would have been easy to start fresh somewhere else, but Mosaic was home, and Mosaic was family. A few years after that leader chose to leave, my husband became the pastor of that same church. *Crazy*, right?

In the early days, when we were all still healing, it was tempting to become like the men holding rocks in John 8. I would have liked to ask God for permission to throw some rocks at the leaders who hurt the community I loved. But given that I didn't humbly speak up about the stank when I first detected it, what could I do but drop my stones and ask for forgiveness instead?

This is the story of every Christian's life: we try to go and sin no more. Invariably, we all wind up with rocks aimed at us for sins we either did or didn't commit. But here's the shocking beauty of this story: being unfairly dragged out and accused before others is sometimes how God heals us. I know this is true because it happened to me. See, grace makes space for Jesus to write in the dirt when one of us messes up.

So where are we, friends, at the end of all this? The church is where we ride shotgun, always in need of the salvation part and occasionally white-knuckling the belonging part. And maybe what's craziest of all is that when you give yourself up to love what Jesus loves, true, real, glorious love starts to spring up and shoot out, all surprising and satisfying. You start saying, like Buddy in the movie *Elf,* "I'm in love, I'm in love, and I don't care who knows it!"[12] I think Paul the apostle sounds a little/a lot like Buddy the Elf as he considers what love for Jesus's bride has done to him:

> Now I rejoice in my sufferings for you, and I am com-
> pleting in my flesh what is lacking in Christ's afflictions
> for his body, that is, the church. I have become its ser-
> vant, according to God's commission that was given
> to me for you, to make the word of God fully known,
> the mystery hidden for ages and generations but now
> revealed to his saints. . . . I labor for this, striving with
> his strength that works powerfully in me. (Col. 1:24–26,
> 29 CSB)

Have you ever praised the price you've paid to love someone else? Ever saluted the saint you've taken a bullet for? Ever thrown a Jesus party over how you suffered for your leader's lack? Paul did. Our ability to love God begins with our willingness to love his messy Bessie church, replete with Goldfish cracker crumbs leaking out of cracked leather and a roof rack that rattles.

I firmly believe and absolutely hope that we can live to see a new kind of day made possible by a new kind of love, the kind of day where Jesus walks out his front door and finds a shiny new

---

[12] *Elf,* directed by Jon Favreau (2003; Burbank, CA: New Line Cinema).

thing built from the stones we could have thrown at each other. I'm fairly convinced this can happen. After all, somehow my grocery getter is still going, and that seems pretty miraculous.

But maybe, to better understand why God loves the church so much, we need to talk about what's under the hood a little. Let's open her up.

CHAPTER 6

Love
in Some Bodies

"To be fond of dancing was a certain step
towards falling in love."

—Jane Austen[1]

When I was in seventh grade, we had to dissect an earthworm in science class. I have since spoken with people who had to dissect frogs and baby pigs and cats, so I grasp that, comparatively speaking, an earthworm is completely banal and no big deal to cut open. But I was a thirteen-year-old girl with a flair for exaggerated drama. Cutting open a worm was a good excuse to make a fuss.

"Waste not, want not," I always say.

Every seventh-grader knows that the key to science lab success is choosing the right partners. I looked around that day and discovered an open seat next to two people I had known since kindergarten. Their names were Robin and Gabriel, and they

---

[1] Jane Austen, *Pride and Prejudice* (Whitehall, UK: T. Egerton, 1813).

spent the majority of our elementary school recesses designing and building habitats for roly-polies.[2] I correctly concluded they would be the kind of partners who would expect zero participation from me.

Looking back, I'm still kind of amazed there are parts to dissect inside one of those tiny, simple worms. The sight of that brown wormy body pinned open to reveal its weird insides is etched in my memory. Gabriel dissected the creature and all its inner stuff. Robin removed and notated the necessary parts. I wrote our names on the lab sheet and squealed when gross stuff came out of the worm. Together, we made up the kind of talented teamwork the world has only witnessed in the 1995 Chicago Bulls, Coco Chanel and her little black dress, the 1927 New York Yankees, and the original cast of *Hamilton*. We were a good team, you guys.

I remembered this seventh-grade version of the CSI lab at the gym the other day. The television in front of my elliptical machine depicted a daytime television show highlighting a dermatologist draining boils and popping pimples. I would have preferred a show about worm dissection.

I hope we can all agree that nature and biology are disgusting. God's creation is majestic and beautiful on the outside but completely repulsive on the inside. If you've spent more than a year fully engaged in any church on the planet, you might know where I'm headed with this thought.

Let's mimic Gabriel's courage (not mine) and cut open the church to see what we're made of. I fully expect to feel the same things I felt all those years ago in the science lab at El Rancho Junior High: a mixture of repulsion, thrill, and awe.

---

[2] Robin went to MIT after high school, and I lost track of Gabriel when he transferred to an elite high school for gifted science students. He probably owns Silicon Valley or something now.

Love in Some Bodies

The First Church

Churches often take on the personality and traits of the person or people who help establish and lead them (church experts call this, unsurprisingly, the "DNA" of a church). If we consider a church to be a community of people who gather to worship, experience, and relate to God, then to look at the first church, we must open our Bibles up to the very beginning and read Genesis 1 and 2.

To understand the first "church," we must open up (or dissect, to use the lab metaphor) and look inside the God who started the church. When we do, we find that, not unlike a lot of what he has made, God's . . . a little weird. Christians have always believed our God is the one true God, while also mysteriously somehow three persons. The first place this three-in-one weirdness pops up is in Genesis 1:26 (CSB) when God said, "Let us make man in our image." Human kings and queens were not the first to use a first-person plural pronoun. The "royal we" is a European knock-off of God's way of chatting with himself as he sat around his divine conference table and made plans.

The Trinity shows up in other places in the bible, such as the baptism of Jesus, where we get all three persons of God in one family snapshot.[3] Or when Jesus commands his disciples in Matthew 28:19 (CSB) to go and "make disciples of all nations, baptizing them in the name of the Father and of the the Son and of the Holy Spirit." Did you catch the oddness of that overly familiar Great Commission? *Hey guys, get out there and baptize people in one name,* Jesus said. *BTW, that one name is Father, Son, and Holy Spirit.*

Jesus struggled with math the same way I struggle with science.[4]

---

[3] Hey, Holy Spirit! Say "cheese!"
[4] Thank you, Mr. Peterson, for trying to help me understand AP physics.

119

Confused by the Trinity? Oddly drawn to it? Me too. So let's dive down the rabbit hole and follow the breadcrumbs that Jesus left us when he prayed his "high priestly prayer":

> I pray not only for these, but also for those who believe in me through their word. May they all be one, as you, Father, are in me and I am in you. May they also be in us, so that the world may believe you sent me. I have given them the glory you have given me, so that they may be one as we are one. I am in them and you are in me, so that they may be made completely one, that the world may know you have sent me and have loved them as you have loved me. (John 17:20–23 CSB)

Somehow, Jesus is *in* the Father, the Father is also *in* Jesus, and Jesus is also *in* us, which all adds up to me being very out of my depth. Of course, we know the Holy Spirit is "up in there" with the Father and Jesus, too. Perhaps that gets us some extra credit points on this spiritual math test. Jesus said all the strange interwoven nature of our spiritual love for one another is the miracle that will prove the gospel to anyone who is brave enough to take a good look at God and ask, *Who all here?*

Theologians use a big, fancy word to describe the mystery of how "three-in-oneness" works. That word is *perichoresis*, and it means "rotation," or, even better, "dance." Am I saying that God is essentially an amazing party with a legit DJ and a dance floor?

Yes. Yes, I am.

All around us, the omnipresent three-in-one God dances, and he has invited us to learn the steps. Maybe this doesn't scare you, because you have rhythm and have mastered all the TikTok dances that exist, but I'm a little intimidated by God's moves because, when presented with a dance to learn, I usually say something like, "I love lamp."

Thankfully, the disciple John had the moves God was looking for to help us follow along.

> What was from the beginning, what we have heard, what we have seen with our eyes, what we have observed and have touched with our hands, concerning the word of life—that life was revealed, and we have seen it and we testify and declare to you the eternal life that was with the Father and was revealed to us—what we have seen and heard we also declare to you, so that you may also have fellowship with us; and indeed our fellowship is with the Father and with his Son, Jesus Christ. We are writing these things so that our joy may be complete.
>
> This is the message we have heard from him and declare to you: God is light, and there is absolutely no darkness in him. If we say, "We have fellowship with him," and yet we walk in darkness, we are lying and are not practicing the truth. If we walk in the light as he himself is in the light, we have fellowship with one another, and the blood of Jesus his Son cleanses us from all sin. (1 John 1:1–7 CSB)

John uses the word *fellowship* to describe the way God moves in us and makes us move in response. Fellowship comes from the word *koinonia*, and it means "a shared participation in relationship." Somehow, John claims, light and life and God are all interconnected, along with all of us. He promises us that if we look at what was from the beginning, at what we have seen and heard, at what past generations have declared concerning the Word of life, we will find our joy made complete. Dissect everything, John tells us, and what you find will bless you more than you can imagine.

The First Body

Let's follow John's advice, return to the beginning of all things, and take a moment to dissect the creation story to see what we can learn. Just as the passages about the Trinity help us understand God better, the original Hebrew language used in Genesis 2 offers insights we might miss when we read only the English words. For example, the Hebrew word for "man" in this passage and the Hebrew word for "ground" are both derived from the word *adamah*, which means "red ground" or "earth." If you really want to geek out on words and meanings, when Genesis 2:7 says that God made man from the dust of the ground, it actually says God made *adam* from *adama*.

Our God is the original green king of recycling and repurposing. When his community-loving heart decided to create a being in his image, he took some good dirt, the Same Old Stuff he had already made, and formed the first man.

But a closer look at the Hebrew in Genesis 2 reveals that while *adam* is translated as "man" in the creation account in Genesis, in many other places in Scripture, it is translated as "mankind." *Strong's Concordance* says the clearest definition for *adam* is "human being."[5] Considering the original Hebrew, we find that the three-persons-in-one God didn't make a "man" first; he simply made a human being, or person, to love God and to be loved by God. This is important when we consider Jesus's prayer in John 17. Humans are uniquely equipped to relate with God because we were first formed in God's image as a created person, and we each derive our unique personhood from God's own three unique divine persons.

But when God created the first person from the stuff, he quickly realized he wasn't finished. All throughout the creation

---

[5]"H120 - 'āḏām – Strong's Hebrew Lexicon (KJV)," Blue Letter Bible, https://www.blueletterbible.org/lexicon/h120/kjv/wlc/0-1/.

process, God repeatedly called his creation good, or *tov* in Hebrew. But when we come to Genesis 2:18, we read that God looked at person and said it was not *tov* for person to be alone.

Given the biblical backdrop of the Trinity, it's easy to imagine our three-persons-in-one God pressing his hands together and interlocking his fingers as he envisioned the perfect community for his creation. Do you remember that little poem from childhood? Someone, usually a Sunday school teacher, made a fist with both hands and stuck up their pointer fingers while saying, "Here is the church, and here is the steeple," then flipped their hands open and wiggled their fingers while saying, "Open the doors, and there are the people." Like a good Sunday school teacher,[6] God held his hands out and said, "Here is the church," but when he flipped his hands over and saw there was just one person sitting on the front row waiting for something to begin, God was like, "Nah, this will never work. You're no good alone."

God Adds Another Person

The idea that aloneness is not good should not surprise us. After all, God is an us, and God's "us-ness" is inside all of us. Humans were made for community because we are made in the image of a communal God who exists in eternal loving fellowship. What was God to do when he realized the first person needed another person to fellowship with? Since a person alone was not *tov*, how could God fix it?

God said that person needed a helper, or an *ezer*. *Ezer* is a beautiful Hebrew word that is often translated as "helper," but it is also a military term, communicating the kind of strong help that

---

[6] Do people still do this? I recall finding the little church I could make with my hands fascinating as a kid. But I think the lack of steeples on our churches these days makes the visual lesson a little less poignant for twenty-first-century children. #whatisasteeple

rescues and saves God's people. We find *ezer* used sixteen times in the Old Testament to describe God as a strong helper. I have listed a few and have highlighted where *ezer* is in each passage below:

- "I am oppressed and needy; hurry to me, God. You are my ***help*** and my deliverer; LORD, do not delay" (Ps. 70:5 CSB—bolded italics mine).
- "There is none like the God of Jeshurun, who rides the heavens to your ***aid***, the clouds in his majesty" (Deut. 33:26 CSB—bolded italics mine).
- "We wait for the LORD; he is our ***help*** and shield" (Ps. 33:20 CSB—bolded italics mine).

An *ezer* is not the kind of help that supports you from behind the scenes or cheers for you from the sideline. An *ezer* runs into your neediness and despair to provide the help and rescue that saves you.

In a very *ezer*-ish move, God rescued person from being alone by providing a flesh-and-blood *ezer*. God put the first human to sleep and pulled out a knife to slice into the Same Old Stuff he used to form the first person. God opened person's body and pulled out some of the Same Old Stuff from inside it. This time, it wasn't dirt and earth; it was bloody bone and flesh that God used to make a new life. God molded the messy insides of the first person to make a second one so that the human community could become a kind of dancing fellowship like God's own.

Together at Last

Our all-knowing God knew that all future human life would spring from that first relationship, including his own life as the Messiah. Sometimes I wonder what it was like for God that day when he split that first body open, exposing the messy insides to create another body destined to procreate generation after generation until, at last, a future descendant would birth Jesus into the world as the Messiah. Can you fathom how the Son felt, watching that Same Old Stuff come out of the first person and make the *ezer*? How did it feel, seeing the first blood exposed on Earth, knowing that his own blood would someday pour out for every descendant of these first people? Every bit of this story causes my heart to swell with love for and awe of God.

In Genesis 2:23 (CSB), the first song about *perichoresis* is sung: "This one, at last, is bone of my bone and flesh of my flesh; this one will be called 'woman,' for she was taken from man."

The first person's song is the first song about *perichoresis*. His lyrics nail the awe-inspiring mystery of being two persons yet made to be one people together. We are overly familiar with the story; it's easy to lose the glory of what he experienced. Can you imagine being alone and asleep in the presence of the God of divine love and then waking up with part of your side missing? The shock alone would knock some of us out again. But then, to turn your head and realize a gorgeous new human is lying beside you. You are in her, and she is in you. It's like . . . spiritual community math magic.

Unless God had held a mirror out for him, the first person had never seen his reflection. He did not know, really, what a human looked like. But he saw her completely. He knew part of his body was in her. He realized they were made of the same God "stuff," and so part of her would always be in him as well.

Once this *ezer* is made, Genesis calls the first person *ish*, which officially means "man," and the second person is called *ishah*, which means "woman." There in the garden, we see the first church flourishing, with man and woman and God in true *koinonia* with each other. *Ishah* came out of *ish*, and both of them were in God while God was also in them. Genesis 2:24 says that this story of mankind's *ezer* being made from the same old messy stuff is the reason a man and a woman become one flesh when they marry. Marriage is the reunification of the two persons who resulted from God's dissection of the first person. When the two become one, they are meant to live in fellowship with God, just as *ish* and *ishah* did before sin entered the world.

But of course, the fellowship got a little sideways one day. *Ish* and *ishah* disobeyed God, and the consequences were tragic. *Ish* named his *ishah* Eve after they sinned, and God sent them away from the tree of life so they wouldn't eat from it and would live forever separated from God's community.

Bless him, God had a plan, because even though people had each other, they didn't have God in the way they needed him. It still wasn't good for people to be alone. There would be another song and another new body someday that would make unity and divine fellowship possible again.

Let's fast forward a few thousand years to a woman named Mary, who lived a very incredible life.

A Second Body

Mary was all alone when the angel Gabriel arrived to tell her some startling but good news. In Luke 1, we can read Gabriel's news that the Holy Spirit would overshadow her and the body of God's own Son would form within her. Lest we assume Mary received her fate as a placid woman with downcast eyes and no emotions at all, let's reconsider this woman whom God asked an awful lot of in life.

In the modern Western world, women who give birth have a relatively low mortality rate. However, according to the World Health Organization, the death rate of pregnant women is much higher in lower income nations.[7] Lack of wealth and access to healthcare results in 94 percent of maternal deaths worldwide

---

[7]"Maternal Mortality," World Health Organization, 19 September 2019, https://www.who.int/news-room/fact-sheets/detail/maternal-mortality.

occurring in those nations. There's no real way to assess the death rate of pregnant women in the ancient world, but we can assume that pregnancy was, at best, precarious for a woman.

God asked Mary to risk her marriage, her social standing, her family's acceptance of her, and her life to carry his Son in her body. God knew this was a lot to ask of one person. Once again, God faced the truth that being alone was not good for people, so Gabriel sent Mary to her cousin Elizabeth for comfort and community.

When Elizabeth greeted Mary, a new song was written in Luke 1. Mary's song is longer than Adam's song, but Adam had only been alive long enough to know he was alone and then he was not. Mary carried generations of trauma and longing within her. She knew the story of God and her people. Mary's knowledge of how desperately they needed rescue is revealed in the words of her song:

> My soul magnifies the Lord,
> and my spirit rejoices in God my Savior,
> because he has looked with favor
> on the humble condition of his servant.
> Surely, from now on all generations
> will call me blessed,
> because the Mighty One
> has done great things for me,
> and his name is holy.
> His mercy is from generation to generation
> on those who fear him.
> He has done a mighty deed with his arm;
> he has scattered the proud
> because of the thoughts of their hearts;
> he has toppled the mighty from their thrones
> and exalted the lowly.
> He has satisfied the hungry with good things

and sent the rich away empty.
He has helped his servant Israel,
remembering his mercy
to Abraham and his descendants forever,
just as he spoke to our ancestors. (Luke 1:46–55 CSB)

Mary's body was the second body God reached into to create life. Her body was made of the Same Old Stuff *ish* and *ishah* were made of, but Mary's body housed a new mystery. Our triune God somehow reached inside himself and sent God the Spirit to overshadow Mary, and then God the Father sent God the Son to form inside Mary's body. The whole Trinity was right there with Mary. The Messiah's body would be born of the Same Old Stuff God had started with at the very beginning of all things. Can you see why John said what was from the beginning can draw us deeper into fellowship with God and one another? We're all made from that Same Old Stuff, too. Crazy, right?

God is always working with the Same Old Stuff. His plans and strategies never change, really. And why should they? Everything he made was good. Creation is a big table of the best potluck dishes ever whipped up. No matter what God scoops out to put on the plate to make things happen, it will be good. Mary understood this. She knew that her holiness and power weren't the forces that would save her on her unconventional path as the mother of the Messiah. She saw her smallness and her lowness but didn't reckon them as liabilities. God himself was her secret weapon, her ace in the hole, her assured promise of safety in an unsafe world.

According to Isaiah's prophetic words about the Messiah in Isaiah 53:2, Jesus grew up to be a not particularly good-looking Jewish man in the ancient world. He began his fully God and fully man life as a tiny baby; but as the years passed, his body matured and became the strong body of a man. He then walked all over

Israel for three years, preaching and teaching and miraculously healing people. Somehow, Jesus's body raised at least three people from the dead. Then his body was arrested, beaten, and hung on a cross.

In Matthew's Gospel, we read that on the day of the crucifixion, from noon until three in the afternoon, the sun was blotted out. The Word that was from the beginning and made all things was suffering and dying. His creation mourned and suffered with him. And then, God the Son, who had never been alone for one moment in all of eternity, cried out in Matthew 27:46 (CSB), "My God, my God, why have you abandoned me?"

The body of one person of the triune God died alone. Jesus willingly allowed himself to be separated from the eternal, divine community. Our God who knew from the very beginning that it wasn't good for people to be alone allowed himself to experience the isolation and abandonment humanity experienced because of sin.

Perhaps divine aloneness caused all the crazy stuff in Matthew 27:50–53. When Jesus died, the curtain in the Jerusalem temple spontaneously tore in half all on its own. Tombs opened up, and dead people emerged and wandered through the city. These details shock us with their impossibility, but since Jesus was the Word made flesh, perhaps they make sense.

If we believe God is who the Bible says he is, then one triune person's separation from the others ought to create some drama in creation, cosmically speaking.

A Third Body

The good news, of course, is that Jesus rose from the dead and appeared in his resurrected body to his followers. The strange news is that God reached into his death to form a third body whose purpose is to make sure no one is ever left alone. That's us, by the way, since we are now the body of Christ, made from the Same Old Stuff. Paul put it like this in Romans 12:4–5 (CSB): "Now as we have many parts in one body, and all the parts do not have the same function, in the same way we who are many are one body in Christ and individually members of one another."

As the church, we are one body, metaphorically speaking. But we are also one body in a physical sense when you consider the way each one of us offers our gifts to help the church function and minister. The story of holy community is the story of how God makes new life by opening up the body. It's the story of blood and bone turned into hope. It's the story of how aloneness is so much worse than the pain of sacrificial love.

These last two years of the pandemic have been painful. In many ways, humanity was ripped open by the pain and trauma. We have been much more alone in a lot of ways. I can't tell you how many times I've personally wanted to quit trying to figure out how to be in community, how to learn new ways to be the church in this new "pandemicky" world. We have been drowning in a soup of bad news, seemingly futile arguments, and poor mental health.

The stories of the people leaving their churches are tragic and heavy. In the midst of arguments over masks and politics and vaccines, we have forgotten that we are in one another. Many of us chose our churches before this worldwide illness because those churches made us feel good for one reason or another. And now nothing makes us feel good, so we are leaving those churches. Many have left the body of Christ when life did not go as expected.

Interestingly, the same thing has happened before.

The disciples had two options when Jesus's body hung and died on a cross. They could give up on him, or they could tend to him. Like the pandemic and politically crushed souls of our day, almost all the first followers of Christ left when the body of Christ was opened up and bled.

But another group didn't leave when Jesus's body was humiliated and unrecognizable.

The women, the *ishahs*, showed up at the tomb of Jesus because they loved this man, even though they didn't think this was how it was supposed to go. It isn't shocking to me that it was women who wouldn't leave Christ's body alone after his death. Nor am I surprised by which women arrived at the tomb to care for the body of Christ. These were *ezers*, and Jesus revolutionized their lives.

Among them was our friend Mary, Jesus's mother. Maternal love and devotion alone would have drawn her to the tomb, but she was also intimately keen to his miraculous being. Next, we have Mary Magdalene, who, according to Luke 8, became a devoted disciple after Jesus healed her and delivered her of evil spirits. Then there was Joanna, the wife of Chuza, and Mary, the mother of James and Joseph. Both had received a miracle from Jesus and responded back with generous care and provision in his life. Why wouldn't their sacrifice and devotion continue after his death? Last, we have Salome, the mother of James and John. Her faith in Jesus as Messiah was absolute during his life. Jesus taught her about the connection between suffering and greatness in Matthew 20. Surely, Salome was at least suspicious that the cross was not the end for Jesus as she packed up the spices and headed for the tomb.

Jesus did the unimaginable for all these women during his life. He scrambled their view of themselves and of God. Jesus allowed them to sit at his feet and learn from him as only men were customarily allowed. These women witnessed Jesus be merciful toward women in adultery and non-Jewish women with sick relatives. They saw him touch women who were considered unclean.

These women knew they were *ezers* because Jesus helped them and rescued them as their *ezer*. The only acceptable place for them was beside the body that had made them come alive, even if it was now dead.

God rewarded the faithful women who arrived at the tomb. Just as *ish* opened his eyes in the garden and glimpsed the first *ishah* to ever rise to her feet, these women were the first people to see our Christ resurrected in all his glory.

Sometimes people will point to the brokenness all around us and say that what the world needs is Jesus. They aren't wrong, exactly, but they are a bit muddled in their diagnosis. The world already has Jesus, as well as God the Father and God the Spirit. Our God is dancing all around us in perfect unity and power. Because we believe God is omnipresent, our problems in life can't be caused by a lack of God's presence in our midst.

What the world needs is people to arise as *ezers*. We need men and women willing to run to the tombs where people have buried their broken hopes and dreams. We need people who will run to the oppressed and mercifully help them see they are made in God's image, out of the Same Old Stuff he uses to make everyone and everything. The world needs a church full of rescuers and strong helpers who will not allow anyone to suffer or die alone.

If your church suffers today, if she seems weary or weak, if she's died and people are burying her, if she seems pregnant but loses too much blood as she labors, perhaps God wants you to run to her and tend her body. Perhaps you are the Martha, Joanna, or Mary who will get to be the first one to see her arise in strength, power, and new life. And please, please know I am not only suggesting this to women readers. God may have strategically put his *ezer*-ness in women, but that doesn't mean a man can't be a strong rescue and help. If a woman can be courageous like Joshua, a loyal friend like Jonathan, and willing to suffer for the gospel like Paul, then surely the men of God in the world can look to bold women of faith as models of God's rescuing presence.

When the word *ezer* was translated as "helpmeet," it tragically came to be understood to mean something akin to "housewife."

We lost the purpose of *ezer*'s creation that ought to inspire both women and men to mirror God's powerful rescue.

So, let's talk about *ezers* for a minute.

How to Be an Ezer

It is tempting, at this point, to tell the stories of some of the great *ezers* in the Bible. Deborah comes to mind, as does Esther. Moses and Joseph fit the profile of rescuers and helpers who defended God's people.

However, to correctly communicate how the church is meant to be an *ezer* in the world, I need to tell you about one *ezer* in particular. She's my grandmother, Lorraine, who we affectionately call Gigi.

Gigi is ninety-three years old and good-naturedly admits she didn't survive this long by being a pushover. If ever there were an *ezer* in the world, my grandmother fits the bill.

Gigi lives in a little house with two other residents, where they have incredible caregivers who treat them like royalty. Recently, a new nurse took over in the afternoons and evenings. His name is Larry, and Gigi adores him. Larry is new to the Austin area. He moved here on a whim of sorts during the pandemic, just to do something new. He didn't know anyone in Austin. Gigi is no stranger to starting over, and she decided Larry needed people. The last time Morgan and I visited Gigi, she told us all about how she had invited Larry to our church. Gigi's love for Larry delighted me as she told us about her conversation with him. She gave him great details about where the church is, where he ought to park, what the entrance to the building would be like, what kind of people he would meet there, how kind everyone would be, what the music would be like, and every other detail she could possibly offer.

"I'm going to keep telling him to go," Gigi said. "He's such a wonderful young man and would be such a great addition to the church."

An *ezer* looks like a person who refuses to leave anyone alone. She looks like one who tirelessly draws the lonely into the greater community because she knows it's not good for people to be alone. But that isn't the only lesson Gigi taught me about being an *ezer*.

When Gigi's youngest son, Tom, was playing youth league baseball several decades ago, Gigi brought a cowbell with her to ring anytime something good happened. She rang the cowbell for Tom when he got a hit or made a play. But she also rang it for the other boys, no matter which team they were on, to celebrate their feats on the field.

There was one particular coach's wife who found the noise of the cowbell unnecessary. This woman went to the coaches to complain, but the coaches seemed to think Gigi had every right to make whatever noise she wanted to make in the stands. Besides, the boys seemed to like it. Not one to be deterred, the woman told Gigi to leave the cowbell at home. Gigi rang her cowbell and suggested the woman return to her seat.

So the woman went to the baseball league board meeting. Gigi "happened" to be at the meeting that night. Gigi also "happened" to have her cowbell in her handbag. After the woman asked the board to ban the cowbell, the head of the board asked who, exactly, rang this much-debated bell. Gigi raised her hand and offered to show him the cowbell if he'd like to see it. He declined. Then he told the woman she had no grounds for complaining and let her know the cowbell would be welcome at the games.

For the remainder of the season, Gigi rang her cowbell at every game. She rang it extra when they played one particular team. I'm sure you can guess which team it was. Decades later, when she turned ninety, we gifted Gigi a new cowbell on her birthday because our family still needs to hear it ring.

The truth is, we all need *ezers* ringing bells around us as they cheer and support and advocate for the greater good. We need them to remind us to celebrate the victories and mourn the losses. Remember, an *ezer* is a strong help and defender; they don't simply go with the flow when someone they love needs rescue. Showing up is a right an *ezer* will not relinquish to the naysayers.

What do cowbells and *ezers* have to do with local churches? I'm so glad you asked.

A Good Body

Unfortunately, we often show up at our churches as spectators, looking for what God's team can do for us. Everybody ultimately loses when the parts of the body of Christ expect the church to solely meet our personal needs by helping us find better jobs, teaching us how to think the right thoughts, improving our families, getting us out of debt, or convincing our kids to remain sexually pure until marriage. When we regard the church as the machine responsible for manifesting the best versions of ourselves and others, we have forgotten that the church is a who, not a what.

Biblically speaking, the church is a person. If Christ is the last Adam, as 1 Corinthians 15:22 explains, then the church is the last Eve. God reached into Jesus's broken and sacrificed body and formed a new person bearing several names, including the body of Christ, the bride of Christ, and the church. Just as your identity, value, and purpose is not solely defined by what you accomplish, the church is much more than what she does. Therefore, although churches involve some of the things on the following list, the church is not meant to be any of these things exclusively:

1. An organization (i.e., a lifeless gathering of entities that exists to equip leaders to fulfill their own self-made goals)
2. A club (i.e., a place for us to all hang out, feel good about ourselves, and meet people)
3. A nonprofit (i.e., a social justice machine, a political think tank, or a platform for making statements about cultural issues)
4. A system (i.e., a structure with hierarchies that limit some people's access to God and/or places of influence)
5. A resource center (i.e., a source for amazing worship, incredible preaching, and perfect programs)
6. A launching pad (i.e., the place where any individual person achieves their dreams of success or power)

The church isn't a place, or a system, or an organization. The church is the final *ezer*, created by God from the broken flesh of the Messiah's body. We would be far less flippant and cynical about how we speak of our churches if we remembered that God reached inside his Son's bloody body and took some of the Same Old Stuff he used to make Adam and Eve and Moses and Elijah and Mary and then used that stuff to make us into the church. When Jesus taught his disciples to take Communion and remember that his body was broken and his blood was spilled so we could become part of the body of Christ, God was trying to make a clear point.

Jesus was the person God opened up so that we and God could be together for an eternity. Just as every bride and groom become one flesh, spiritually speaking, Jesus and his church share a body here on earth. We are the parts of that body, and our strong, determined, enduring, *ezer*-fueled love for one another is the lifeblood of the body of Christ.

How will we tend the body we share with our savior today? Will we scorn it for being wrong about so many things, and will we take the sharp edge of a tweet to her flesh and cut her open just a little? Will we try to cut off the parts of her body who voted in a way we don't like or don't understand, and will we lose the benefit of connected fellowship and diverse belonging? Will we abuse her body, objectifying her into a platform to promote our own brand? Will we wordlessly abandon one local church for failing us and take our same expectations to a new church without examining our own hearts?

I hope not.

Father, help us to hold and cherish your Son's bride when she fails us the same way you have held and cherished us when we have failed you. Spirit, remind us of all the ways you have given us new life in this body by connecting us with people we don't always understand. Jesus, remind us that you deemed every person who makes up the body of Christ worthy of your own bodily sacrifice.

God, our great *ezer*, is up there in the stands. He's ringing his cowbell in celebration of the joy he feels to be at our game, watching us play.

Let's go win.

Part Three

Tacos

Sharing Together in Our Common Mission

Answering God's Missional Call

CHAPTER 7

Tacos
as an Ancient E-vite

"No one achieves anything alone."

—Leslie Knope[1]

ay back in the Introduction, I mentioned that tacos would serve as a working metaphor for our discussion of God's mission in the world. Before we dive into our tacos (oy, how I love to dive into a plate of tacos!), I'd like to briefly chat about the word *mission* to get us all on the same page. The topic of mission has gained some real traction in recent discussions about church and Christian spirituality. The missional movement changed many of our perspectives about living out our faith. A "mission" is no longer a trip to a developing part of the world. A "mission" is no longer a very old

---

[1] *Parks and Recreation*, season 4, episode 22, "Win, Lose, or Draw," aired May 10, 2012, on NBC.

stucco building, filled with swallows, somewhere in California.[2] It is no longer ministry performed somewhere far away only by professional "missionaries." For many followers of Jesus, the idea of Christian mission has developed into demonstrating our faith and allegiance to God and to his love for the world with our behavior and activism in whatever context we might find ourselves.

Or, put more succinctly, missional living means getting stuff done for needy, wounded, and/or oppressed people.

People seem to respond differently to the concept of living on mission, though. Some of us are thrilled by the idea that God has called us to live on mission in our neighborhoods, cities, and nation. Any excuse to go and do something for God seems like permission to flex. The awesomeness we achieve, however, may be determined by whether we're capable of being missional as well as being kind and wise. Unfortunately, those three characteristics don't always live together in unity.

Others of us are intimidated by all talk of pursuing a missional life. Perhaps we have seen people we love burn out as they tried to be the hands or feet of Christ. Maybe our personality or some trauma we've endured makes us skittish of knocking on a neighbor's door, joining a team of people at a shelter, or flying to a city ravaged by poverty to offer aid.

Any discussion of God's call to mission is an inherently uncomfortable space. But the first step into mission doesn't have to involve jumping off a cliff or a near-spiritual-death experience. For our purposes, we'll start with a hot August walk my daughter and I took through our church parking lot.

On that particular summer Saturday, my daughter and I were at church because she had a dance rehearsal for a special

---

[2] If you grew up in California, you most likely built a to-scale model of San Juan Capistrano at some point in your life. Or at least your parents made it, and then you turned it in. #survivorstories

back-to-school Sunday morning. We weren't there for any real missional purpose, but other people were. In fact, a large crowd had gathered under several tents in the parking lot, seeking respite from the blazing Texas Sun as they offered and received service and care.

I saw my friend Leah deep in conversation with a woman worn down from street life. Not far from them, homeless people were queued up, awaiting guidance regarding Texas identity cards, grocery store gift cards, prescription glasses, and other necessities. Good Texas barbecue beckoned from the food line. Church volunteers and nonprofit organizers bustled amid the laughter of the crowd, chatting as they wrote down requests or passed out what was available. This was a typical Saturday at our church; the day teams of volunteers who serve the homeless of our city gather and get stuff done. While no one was actually passing out tacos that day, everything in that parking lot looked spiritually delicious. I love a good food metaphor, and tacos are as good as any meal you can ever hope to find.

After all, who doesn't like tacos of some kind? No matter what you're hungry for, a taco could probably satisfy your craving. Crispy, soft, *al carbon*, fish, vegetarian, breakfast, and dessert variations all exist in delicious glory. If you don't believe me, come to Austin. In this city, everyone loves some version of you-name-it-we-can-put-it-on-a-tortilla. Tacos are the food you make when you invite too many of your friends over for dinner. They're comfort food that is also colorful and can be served in an assembly-line style, which invariably feels a little like a party.

Looking at the bustle in the church parking lot that day with my daughter, I saw spiritual tacos being passed out all over the place. We walked past people feasting on laundry tacos, new jeans tacos, shower tacos, government paperwork tacos, health-care tacos, and haircut tacos. Strange as it may seem, I've come to think of missional acts of love and care and rescue as just that—spiritual tacos.

If this idea of describing spiritual acts with tasty food metaphors seems familiar to you, it may be because Jesus used food metaphors to describe how God takes care of people, too. In Luke 14:15 (CSB), Jesus said, "Blessed is the one who will eat bread in the kingdom of God!" Then he told his disciples a parable about a man who wanted to throw a big party, but no one wanted to come. The Bible says all his friends and acquaintances made excuses. Were their reasons valid? The Bible doesn't say for sure. Maybe his would-be guests thought they were too good for his party. Perhaps he wasn't serving the kind of food they liked best. For some reason, they thumbed their nose at his invitation. So, the man had his servants go out to the streets to find guests among the poor and needy, and he filled his house with anyone hungry enough to show up and eat what he offered. What is Jesus telling us here about the bread in the kingdom of God and the party God's throwing?

God isn't choosy about who joins the party, so long as they're hungry and willing to leave their cares and worries behind. When God invites people to abide in his kingdom, he offers his guests spiritual food and holy friendship. In the New International Tex-Mex Version[3] of Luke 14:15, Jesus's words sound like this: *Blessed is the one who will eat the tacos at God's taco party.*

Allow me to extend the missional taco party metaphor momentarily: our allegiance to Jesus's authority is the wristband that gets us in the door of the whole thing. Grace and truth-filled church communities are the main venues where God's party guests gather. And an elaborately arranged dinner display awaits, where God's faithful servants offer God's spiritual tacos to everyone he's invited. But what are these portable expressions of God's heart supposed

---

[3] This is not an actual version of the Bible. ;)

to be filled with? What are we supposed to taste when we sink our teeth into mission?

Jesus's famous sermon from Matthew 5 can help answer that question. While some say it's the greatest sermon ever preached, I like to think of it as an ancient e-vite to his party.

Blessed are the poor in spirit,
> for the kingdom of heaven is theirs.
Blessed are those who mourn,
> for they will be comforted.
Blessed are the humble,
> for they will inherit the earth.
Blessed are those who hunger and thirst for righteousness,
> for they will be filled.
Blessed are the merciful,
> for they will be shown mercy.
Blessed are the pure in heart,
> for they will see God.
Blessed are the peacemakers,
> for they will be called sons of God.
Blessed are those who are persecuted because of righteousness,
> for the kingdom of heaven is theirs.
You are blessed when they insult you and persecute you and falsely say every kind of evil against you because of me. Be glad and rejoice, because your reward is great in heaven. For that is how they persecuted the prophets who were before you. (Matt. 5:3–12 CSB)

Jesus found himself in front of a big crowd that day, and he listed off all the ingredients on the menu at his party: comfort, blessing, fullness, mercy, a glimpse of something or someone powerful, and (more than anything) a place to belong.

This Trinity taco bar isn't ultimately about the tacos, though. God's missional intention in the world has never been merely about handing stuff out. Nor is God's primary goal to create a more safe or comfortable world for his people. This becomes uncomfortably clear in Matthew 5 when Jesus spills the party tea and lets us know that there are some spicy ingredients in his tacos, like insults, slander, and persecution.

Jesus said God invites and then rewards the empty, the needy, and the persecuted. However, when we list all the things humans dream of being in life, empty, needy, and persecuted are firmly placed at the bottom of the list. At the center of Christianity is a clear message: if we dump the world's gifts and ideals out on the ground and show up before God empty-handed, we can expect a kind of reward the wealthiest, most-popular people on Earth could never offer anyone.

The God of love has offered himself to us in the same way each of the three persons of God eternally offer themselves to one another. In the eternal, joyous, rotational relationship of the God persons, we see the way God equates love with giving oneself to another person. God loves himself by giving himself. Jesus's words show us this principle—that giving oneself involves either obedience and submission, or sacrificing one's life:

> As the Father has loved me, I have also loved you. Remain in my love. If you keep my commands you will remain in my love, just as I have kept my Father's commands and remain in his love.
>
> I have told you these things so that my joy may be in you and your joy may be complete.
>
> This is my command: Love one another as I have loved you. No one has greater love than this: to lay

down his life for his friends. You are my friends if you
do what I command you. (John 15:9–14 CSB)

Our triune God is self-loving and self-giving. The Father loved
the world by sending the Son to save us (John 3:16). The Son of
God loved his followers by sending the Spirit to testify to us (John
15:26). The Holy Spirit loves the Father and the Son by remaining
here with God's people, empowering us to be Christ's witnesses
(Acts 1:8).

God's tacos are stuffed with the love of the sending Father, the
sacrificial Son, and the empowering Spirit. Once eaten, the spicy
truth in those tacos stays with us to remind us that God's will is
for us to be self-loving and self-giving, just as he is.

As counterintuitive as it sounds, responding to God's missional
call begins with attempting to balance self-love and self-giving.

Before you accuse me of making stuff up about God, allow me
to direct you to Matthew 19:16–19, where a young, rich, powerful
man asked Jesus what he had to do to earn eternal life. Jesus told
him he needed to keep the commandments; and when the young
man asked for specifics, Jesus replied with this: "Do not murder;
do not commit adultery; do not steal; do not bear false witness;
honor your father and your mother; and love your neighbor as
yourself" (Matt. 19:18–19 CSB). Look at Jesus, coming in hot and
setting my whole house on fire. All God requires is for me to perfectly obey God's law *and* love my neighbor the same way/to the
extent that I love *myself*? Lord, have mercy.[4]

Self-love is a tricky space to hold as a Christian in the modern
world. We're used to hearing "Love God; love others" as a Christian
missional mantra of sorts. And while it's good and true that we
need to love God and others, it can become an incomplete sentiment if we forget how Jesus said to measure our love. We should

---

[4] Literally, have mercy on me and help me do this, God.

probably say, "Love God; love yourself; love others," but I think we're afraid of getting stuck in the land of Love Yourself. However, Jesus said the love we offer others is meant to be portioned out equally to the love we give to ourselves.

There is a clear biblical principle at work here in Matthew 19, yet Christians rarely talk about the value of self-love. Even in this era of increasing awareness of good mental health, few of us are comfortable espousing great love and care for ourselves. But when we ground our self-love in the love God offers himself and us, we begin to see that holy self-love is simply agreeing with what God has already declared about our worth.

Without a proper understanding of why we are personally worthy of love, we will never fully grasp why others deserve it. It's not wrong to love yourself; it's just wrong for our self-love to be out of balance with our willingness to lovingly give ourselves to God and others.

If no one has told you today, God really, really, really, really likes you. He appreciates your unique talents and gifts. He loves your loud and (sometimes) hilarious jokes, and he loves your quiet and tender words. He loves the way that one pair of shoes makes you feel fancy so you walk with some swagger. God likes how you make space for others in your life, the way you text your friends, and how you take care of yourself when you have a bad day. One of God's favorite things is seeing you be the friend to yourself that God knows you need. His other favorite thing is seeing you reach out for friendship from others when you've run out of energy or provisions to take care of yourself.

God the Father has never once regretted loving you enough to be willing to give his Son to save you. God the Son has never rued the day he died to save you. God the Spirit has never resented your intense and deep need for him. Not ever—not even once. Not when you messed up. Not when you fell down. Not when you were angry or petty or frustrated or dumb about stuff. He's always had another second chance waiting for you, even when you didn't need it. God's love is big like that—full of grace, mercy, and forgiveness.

You're one of God's favorite people, which is why he wants you to give yourself to others. God wants everyone in your life to experience the same joy he experiences in his relationship with you. And while this means you're special to God, here is the unfathomable truth: everyone is that special to God, and God wants all people to love themselves so they can grasp the value of their love and friendship in this world.

To find the delight God feels for all of us, I like to remind myself that God's in a good mood today because he has us, and he has a plan. God is keenly aware of the injustice and pain we face in the world, and he is encouraged by his brilliant plan to meet those needs by calling his people to complete his will and bring his love and wholeness (aka those spiritual tacos) to a broken world. And in this wide world we live in, God uses one language above all others to tell us about his plan. Let's talk about love languages for a second, okay?

God's Love Language

Back in 2001, I got married, and Gary Chapman wrote *The 5 Love Languages*. Morgan and I attended a church marriage retreat two weeks after our wedding, where we took a test to determine our love languages. Because we were astonishingly poor back then, I felt personally attacked by all the talk of love languages[5] after my test results revealed I received love in the form of meaningful and (unfortunately) expensive gifts. Many of our early arguments

---

[5] Mean girls like Regina George (of *Mean Girls* fame) have nothing on Gary Chapman and his personal attacks, in my opinion.

involved me crying for pretty things while Morgan tore his clothes and gnashed his teeth.[6]

To prove how little I've matured since my midtwenties, I offer this conversation from last week, which occurred while Morgan and I enjoyed a long walk through our neighborhood:

Morgan: What can I do to help you feel more loved?
Me: A new car would be nice. And maybe a pool.
Morgan: No, but really . . .
Me: Maybe you could go fishing, and you'll find a hundred thousand dollars in a fish's mouth like Jesus did that one time.
Morgan: . . . or maybe I could change some light bulbs and take your car to get the oil changed.
Me: Sounds good.

The next night, after the dead light bulbs were swapped for good ones and the car was ready to go, thirty adults and children gathered in our small backyard for our church community group. We have met alfresco ever since the pandemic came in like a wrecking ball. A folding table holds our potluck dinner, and everyone scooches into a circle in folding lawn chairs. A few years ago, this setup would have left me aghast. The need for mosquito spray alone would have horrified me. But after a lonely lockdown, we are different people.[7]

Seventeen months of Zoom gatherings left us hungry for face-to-face fellowship. Many of us are vaccinated; some of us are not. Some of us have had Covid; many of us have not. Masks and outside air keep us safe from possible health risks while our

---

[6] After over twenty years of marriage, our arguments just involve one of us saying, "I know I'm probably wrong, but you're being a jerk," the other person saying, "Okay," and then just trying again.

[7] The true gift of the pandemic: lower standards for fellowship with higher standards for clean hands.

time together reminds us to love one another well, no matter what response we have chosen regarding the current health crisis.

After we took turns sharing short life updates that night, we prayed for one another. As I looked around at the bowed heads, it occurred to me that the perimeter of our circle would make the perfect shape for our backyard pool. What a poignant gift God threw my way that night.

"Show me your love in the form of a pool," I had jokingly told my husband. But here we all were, a people swimming in God's love and community. I realized then, twenty years after reading *The 5 Love Languages*, that while God communicates many loving truths through gifts, words of affirmation, physical touch, quality time, and acts of service, none of these is God's primary love language.

God's love language is *people*. In the same way that you feel loved when you get that compliment or that I (would) feel loved when I (one glorious day) get that pool, God feels loved when we, his already people, invite more people to his taco party to be loved.

This is what Jesus was getting at before turning things over to his disciples in Matthew 28. He gathered his already people and said the entire point of him having all authority in heaven and on Earth was, in fact, bringing in more people.

> All authority has been given to me in heaven and on
> earth. Go, therefore, and make disciples of all nations,
> baptizing them in the name of the Father and of the Son
> and of the Holy Spirit, teaching them to observe every-
> thing I have commanded you. And remember, I am with
> you always, to the end of the age. (Matt. 28:18–20 CSB)

In a way, Jesus asked us to find more people and teach them about the Trinity by baptizing them in the name of the one God who is three persons. Jesus wanted everyone to know this whole thing is about many being one. Then he commanded us to remember that he's always with us.

Seen through this lens, God's mission is about making sure no one is left alone, and it's accomplished wherever we gather in a purposeful effort to draw more people into the dance of the triune community of God.

And now, as we dance around one another, learning to empty ourselves and give away what God has blessed us with, we spin toward the possibility that God will send us to fill someone *and* send someone to fill us. People are not exclusively "missionaries" or "missional targets." We are both at the same time. We are full of need and full of provision.

How can this be?

A shocking, nasty, and brilliantly hopeful story hidden in a corner of 2 Kings narrates how these twin needs of giving and receiving intersect to become a conduit of mission.

Bad Skin, Good Deeds

If you're unfamiliar with 2 Kings, let me set the scene a bit. Elisha was the super awesome prophet (or the S.A.P.) for Israel at that point in history. As we begin reading in 2 Kings chapter 7, we must understand that he'd had a terrible time of late. Israel was at war with Aram, and in chapter 6, Elisha correctly predicted every move the Arameans made in their attempt to defeat Israel. So the Arameans tried to attack Israel and capture Elisha. Israel's king wanted to massacre the attackers, but Elisha had mercy on them. He said to feed them and send them home. (Please notice: Elisha was way ahead of his time here, living out the call in Matthew 5 to be merciful and love our enemies.)

Later, Aram besieged the city and caused a terrible famine. Some Israelites suffered so much that they ate their children. Israel's king grieved his nation's suffering, cursed God, and blamed

Elisha. A man of action, he sent an executioner to kill Elisha.[8] Elisha promptly locked his door and informed the executioner that the famine would end in twenty-four hours.

God had a plan to save his people, but it would not be the S.A.P. who would save them all. Their deliverer would emerge through quite a plot twist. Have you noticed how much our God loves an underdog? The unlikely hero is God's favorite story. The unlikely hero holding a plate of spiritual tacos is his masterpiece.

In 2 Kings 7:3, we are introduced to four unlikely heroes holding four unlikely plates. This Israelite quartet of lepers were cast out of the city because their skin showed signs of disease. As I read this passage today, I could hear God asking us this question: Would you accept a taco Tuesday invitation from four sick and potentially contagious people? Because that's what happened next.

Physically, these men were food-deprived, which was terrible. However, everyone was hungry then. That's what a famine produces: hunger. But in addition to starving, these men suffered even more because of the law about lepers. According to the instructions in Leviticus 13:45–46, lepers were required to stay separated from their friends and families until their skin disease was healed. They were also required to wear torn clothing, leave their hair unbrushed, cover their mouths, and shout the word "Unclean!" if anyone approached them. Relationally and socially, these four men were skin and bones.

With nothing to live for, they hatched a crazy plan and rolled the dice. The lepers left their people and went to surrender themselves to the Arameans. They hoped for some food and perhaps the chance to live. But as they headed toward the Aramean camp, the Lord did something miraculous. He caused the Arameans to hear the sound of a large army approaching (like teenagers coming

---

[8] Everybody's solution to confronting Elisha was always death. What's the deal with that?

down the stairs, only slightly less terrifying). Aram's army abandoned their camp because they thought they would be conquered.

By the time the hungry lepers arrived, the empty camp welcomed them with abundant food and treasures. They filled their stomachs first and then gathered and hid silver, gold, and clothing for themselves. But in 2 Kings 7:9 (CSB), the well-fed and newly wealthy lepers grew a conscience. "Then they said to each other, 'We're not doing what is right. Today is a day of good news. If we are silent and wait until morning light, our punishment will catch up with us. So let's go tell the king's household.'"

Where did these lepers get the idea that the right thing to do was to go and be merciful? Who taught them to feed the very people who had decided they deserved shunning and death? This is incredible and unheard of. *Go share with the ones who cast you out.* Where did they learn this? Most likely, they learned this from Elisha. Surely they had heard how Elisha, in an extraordinary stroke of mercy, had fed the Aramean enemies who came to capture him.

Long before Luke recorded his version of the Sermon on the Mount and reported that Jesus said to bless those who curse you, to turn the other cheek when someone slaps you, and to love your enemies, Elisha modeled a life of blessing and feeding those in places of power who have persecuted you. Elisha knew God desired mercy most of all, long before Jesus said he chose to eat with sinners and sellouts because God desired mercy more than sacrifice.

The lepers had Elisha as their example, and he was good, but we have someone far better. We have a great and holy high priest who offered himself to save us from the spiritual famine created by our sin. While Elisha chose mercy, despite the risk it brought to his own life, Jesus took mercy one step further. While those lepers chose to share the bounty of the abandoned camp with people who had cast them out and despised them, Jesus chose to share the bounty of heaven with the people who stood by and watched him be executed.

The hope in God's heart has always been a simple one: that the people he created would accept the invite to his party, join his dance, and learn to receive and serve spiritual tacos. We are the lepers God sent to bring God's rescue to a suffering world. We are the sheep of God's pasture who hear his voice and obey his call to go and make disciples. We are the delicious offerings God is handing out to a world looking for satisfaction in all the wrong places.

Mission in the Urban Dictionary

Can I be vulnerable for a moment? All this talk of mercy and mission has me wondering if I should up my mission game a bit.[9] Nothing makes you reassess your wardrobe like realizing you're invited to a big-deal party, and God's invitation to join him in loving and serving has me side-eyeing the missional acts hanging in my closet. I warned at the beginning of this chapter that talking about mission is uncomfortable. Well, I've even made myself quite uncomfortable and feel compelled to question every missional detail of my life.

Should I volunteer at my daughter's school as a crossing guard? Should I increase our financial support to missionaries? Will I understand Jesus, the church, and the call to live on mission better if I stretch myself further than I am already stretched, give more time or money than I am already giving, or sacrifice some privilege I have taken for granted?

The needs of the world are an awful lot like the laundry of our family of six: there is always more that can be done.

---

[9] Nothing makes you feel like you should do more to love God and others better like writing a book about how to love God and others better. #clingingtograce

But when I look at the world through the lens of mission as God's call to be self-loving and self-giving, the pressure to always do more quiets down. I sense a holy hush in our midst when I consider that God doesn't use the quantity of need left in the world to judge our missional efforts. We can release the compulsion to equate mission with a scoreboard of any kind, and we can instead intentionally receive and give love as a people who were made for love.

Because God's missional will in the world is that all people would experience the kind of love and care they deserve as people made in his image, any act we participate in that provides evidence that God rules, reigns, saves, heals, comforts, and empowers is the work of God's mission in the world. Any love we offer to end injustice and heal the pain created by racism, classism, poverty, and ableism is beautiful work.

Listening to the worries our children carry is God's mission. Checking in on our friends when they're struggling is God's mission. Volunteering at a shelter, inviting a neighbor to dinner, giving money to aid organizations, becoming a foster parent, picking up trash at a local park, genuinely asking a friend about their faith and sharing about your faith in return, supporting missionaries, praying for leaders in all sectors of society, raising money to go on a mission trip, organizing church retreats, rescuing neglected animals, and offering to loan your car to someone when they need it are all examples of how we can engage in God's mission.

I have called our acts of mission "tacos" because the image of Jesus handing us tacos to pass out seems more doable than meeting the deep needs of the whole world. The idea of a missional life easily unnerves us. Human hearts can rebel against reminders of how we ought to prioritize justice done in the public square. I can't exactly explain it, but somehow, even when we reach out and try to meet the needs of others, we can be left with a deep sense of our ineffective smallness.

Yesterday, I told someone dear to me, someone who has loved me and ministered to me, that I knew they loved me as much as God does. This statement made my friend uncomfortable.

"I don't know about that," they said. "But I've loved you as much as I can."

I considered these words for a moment and then said, "I'm pretty sure that's exactly how much God loves me, too. Maybe that's how he measures love. Not in quantitative amounts, but according to our willing generosity."

I believe that's how God measures missional effort, too. Do we show up willing and generous when he invites us to the party? If the answer to that is "Yes," well, then we've done as much as he expects of us. This is, without a doubt, a good reason to throw a big party. Of course, sometimes parties are costly and a little painful to get through.[10] Can we cry if we want to at God's taco party? I think we can, and possibly, the tears may be unavoidable.

---

[10] Introverts know a lot about how painful big parties can be.

Tacos
Full of Pain

"No question about it. I am ready to get hurt again."[1]

—Michael Scott

I am the kind of person who embraces pain relief the same way a shy toddler wraps her arms around her mother's legs when introduced to a stranger. That is to say, I want to hug pain relief medicine to prove my appreciation for it. I find immense comfort in the idea that ibuprofen can help me through the inevitably vulnerable moments of suffering that remind me I am human. The occurrence of these kinds of moments increases steadily as my midlife body finds new ways to stop working properly.

Last week, I woke up and dared to stand up out of bed immediately, which caused an immediate back spasm because middle

---

[1] *The Office*, season 4, episode 10, "Branch Wars," aired November 1, 2007, on NBC.

age has come to claim me. I was grateful for ibuprofen that day. Life is too painful, from both a physical and an existential perspective. I wish Walgreens sold ibuprofen for self-esteem during days when publishers reject my book proposals or my kids notice I look nothing like the person in my wedding photos.[2]

When I "fell pregnant,"[3] as they used to say, and I began to plan the birth of our first baby, I was team epidural all the way. If it had been available, I would have signed up for a mobile epidural machine to wheel around behind me for trips to Target. But sometime in my second trimester, a friend suggested I pray about a birth plan.[4] This seemed holy and quite Christian-ish. I enthusiastically set about proving I was serious about God, his will, and all the mom things. However, as I prayed one day, I began to question getting an epidural, which was obviously ridiculous. Medicine is God's gift to us! Along with central air and running water, pain medicine is one of the perks of modern life. I was born to birth babies here in the twenty-first century, not in the eighteenth century when women had to bear down and try not to notice that no one could help them at all.

The more I prayed about it, the more God reassured me that, despite being a modern woman, I still should not get an epidural. He then squashed my soul with a warning that my birthing destiny would include an episiotomy.[5] I tried talking God into a *Star Trek* "Beam me up, Scotty" birth instead. I reminded him of the story in

---

[2] Although they don't completely numb the pain in these moments, powdered donuts brighten the dark days of reality and rejection. Five stars for sure.

[3] I'd love to know the history of this phrase. Actually, strike that. It's probably from some horrible ancient practice of pushing women down hills after a betrothal ceremony or something. Let's just keep moving along, shall we?

[4] The whole idea of a birth plan is peachy, except that they are often pointless exercises whose sole purpose is to trick our psyches into believing we have some control over the uncontrollable revolution happening in our bodies.

[5] If you don't know what an episiotomy is, don't Google it. Just keep moving through this story. Knowledge is not always power.

Acts 8 when he beamed Philip from the road to Gaza all the way to the town of Azotus. I promised that if he beamed my baby out of me, I would wear a "Won't he do it!" shirt every day for at least a year and tell everyone who asked about my shirt the story of my baby's miraculous birth. It seemed like a great marketing strategy for God, IMHO. But I guess God either isn't a big *Star Trek* fan, or he felt that he didn't need another influencer on his "Won't he do it" campaign, because he clearly said, "No epidural," and then I guess God went to make a sandwich because he was done chatting with me and needed to get on with his day.

I tend to obey God when he twists my arm like that, so I didn't get the epidural when the birthing day arrived. Contractions came and went and came and went, and the baby stayed stuck in one spot. Eventually, the doctor helped him enter the real world with a big suction machine.[6] About twenty minutes later, I laid in the bed, tenderly holding my son, wholly exhausted and determined that we would adopt all future progeny.

Suddenly, Morgan noticed the baby's lips were turning blue. He had stopped breathing. We watched in shock as a dozen nurses and doctors flooded the room to resuscitate our baby. Later, it was explained that birth is traumatic for babies who get stuck in the womb.[7] Being stuck in limbo between the womb and the world for three hours is particularly hard on new little humans who have never breathed air before, so they sometimes forget to keep breathing after they're born.

When I checked in at the hospital on that fateful day seventeen years ago, my delivery nurse initially seemed a little peeved that I didn't want an epidural. Women in pain require more care,

---

[6] Please imagine this like some kind of Bugs Bunny cartoon, because that is how I have always pictured it since I really had no idea what was going on down there.

[7] I wanted to point out that it's not exactly a day at the spa for the birth mother, but I held my tongue.

I suppose. But in the end, she told me that not having the epidural had been an important factor that day. Just before they wheeled me away to a recovery room, she casually mentioned that my decision not to get the epidural had probably helped me push more effectively.

"Pain helps you know when to push. You probably would have had to deliver him C-section if you'd had an epidural," she told me.

I have no grudge against C-sections. I have many friends who sing their praises, and any reasonable method for getting unpregnant after nine months of carrying an increasingly growing human being inside my body sounds like heaven to me. But what neither I nor my nurse knew that fateful day in 2004 was that my motherhood story was about to get a tad . . . hectic. God had big plans to surprise me with another baby in 2005 and then another one in 2006. Three C-sections in twenty-seven months isn't ideal for anyone's uterus. Would my body have been able to handle a fourth C-section when baby number four came in 2008? Possibly. But I'm grateful we didn't have to find out.

Any time showing up to the party ready to love and serve sacrificially has involved pain, my nurse's words have returned to me over the years. *Pain helps us push more accurately.* In the world of spiritual growth, we feel this truth any time we engage in spiritual practices like fasting, tithing, or silence. There in the pain of sacrifice, we surrender to a truth higher than our drive toward self-preservation. The physical and psychological discomfort involved in spiritual practices heightens our awareness of where God needs us to push so that life can be birthed in new ways, both within ourselves and in the world beyond.

What exactly do pain and birthing have to do with God's mission in the world? I'm so glad you asked. Let's talk about our daddy momma God, shall we?

Our Daddy Momma

Interestingly, procreating and giving birth was the first missional call God ever gave to humans. This doesn't necessarily mean that parenting is somehow the highest missional call in a Christian's life, but this fact does reveal God's high value of new life. Jesus and the apostles used birth and infancy as metaphors for God's mission in our lives and the world. Consider the following passages:

- "Jesus replied, 'Truly I tell you, unless someone is born again, he cannot see the kingdom of God'" (John 3:3 CSB).
- "'Truly I tell you,' he said, 'unless you turn and become like little children, you will never enter the kingdom of heaven'" (Matt. 18:3 CSB).
- "Jerusalem, Jerusalem, who kills the prophets and stones those who are sent to her. How often I wanted to gather your children together, as a hen gathers her chicks under her wings, but you were not willing" (Luke 13:34 CSB)!
- "Blessed be the God and Father of our Lord Jesus Christ. Because of his great mercy he has given us new birth into a living hope through the resurrection of Jesus Christ from the dead" (1 Pet. 1:3 CSB).
- "Like newborn infants, desire the pure milk of the word, so that by it you may grow up into your salvation, if you have tasted that the Lord is good" (1 Pet. 2:2–3 CSB).
- "Dear friends, let us love one another, because love is from God, and everyone who loves has been born of God and knows God" (1 John 4:7 CSB).

Through these scriptures (and others like them), we understand that the Christian story is one of a Father God who sent his Son on mission into the world to give spiritual birth to God's children through the Holy Spirit. Many books and sermons of the past have done an incredible job of teaching us about what it means to have a good Father God. However, because our God gives birth (Peter's words, not mine), it is sound and biblical, especially as we consider what it means to embrace God's mission, to regard God as a holy and divine mother as well.

And how do many mommas roll?

I sometimes joke that my role as a mother is to act as a sump pump in our family. Somehow, despite having responsible children and an involved, intentional partner in my husband, I tend to wind up knee-deep in everyone's flooded metaphorical basements, pumping out the consequences of their mistakes, messes, and catastrophes. As toddlers, my children woke me up, not my husband or each other, when they felt afraid or sick in the middle of the night. They felt free to challenge me most often as wily elementary-age people, testing boundaries and questioning parental authority. These days, I am the parent my teens reach out to with their scary teenage confessions and questions late at night. I recognize this is a generalization and therefore not always true, but mothers are often reliable places to run to when a kid is eyebrow-deep in stuff they can't handle.

Why? Good mothers of the world long for their children to be safe. Good mothers fight for their children to be rescued. Good mothers teach children what to do when they are in danger or afraid. Biblically speaking, this stems from the creation of woman as an *ezer*. A momma is a source of strong and mighty relational rescue, first and foremost.

Mister Rogers once famously explained in an interview that his mother told him to look for the helpers during a catastrophe. "If you look for the helpers, you'll know that there's hope," Rogers emphasized.[8] I don't know if she meant to tell her son to look for *ezers* when life got scary, but essentially, that was what she did.

---

[8] Fred Rogers Interview Part 3 of 9, Television Academy Foundation, July 22, 1999, https://interviews.televisionacademy.com/interviews/fred-rogers.

Mrs. Rogers simultaneously created a value for being a helper when others are in distress, and we have her to thank for much of the love and safety *Mister Rogers' Neighborhood* offered the children of the world for all those years.

But rescue is not the only attribute of God that we often see mirrored in earthly mothers. Like God, mommas of the world get stuff done.

Multitasking and Expectations

Any mother will tell you that their life requires first class, PhD-level multitasking skills. Whether those skills come naturally to a mother is entirely beside the point. If a baby wakes up from a nap hungry in the middle of an older sibling's bath time, the mother must hold the baby and finish bathing the toddler. If a toddler's stomach gets upset during a car trip, a mother must keep her cool, explain what to do with vomit, and continue to drive until it's safe to pull over. If two twins are hungry at the same time, a mother must figure out how to feed both at once or feed one while distracting the other. If a mother gets a call from an anxious teen in the middle of a sibling's volleyball game, the mother must cheer for one child while counseling the other. If a mother gets a call from the school regarding a bullying incident in which her child is the bully minutes before an important meeting with a client, the mother must look confident, cool, and collected despite her internal drive to either defend or attack her child.

To all the mothers out there on mission in their kids' lives, sump-pumping the rotten water out of their lives, attempting to offer tasty spiritual tacos despite their children's immature choices, and juggling far too many responsibilities and needs than you can meet, I'd like to reassure you that God sees your sacrifice. He, too, is a sump pump/taco maker/juggler extraordinaire who can help you when your arms are too weak or when the days become tedious.

Busy mommas are a stellar metaphor for a person answering a broader call to God's mission in the world. A personified sump pump cooking tacos while juggling is an excellent word picture of missional life. Just as most mothers grapple with insecurity about whether or not they're doing enough for their children, all our insecure feelings about successfully maintaining a missional life are rooted in the impossibility of executing the details of missional life well.

There are no perfect moms, and there are no perfect missionaries.

To start a revolution in your own inner life, repeat these words as often as possible: *God does not expect me to perfectly meet every need I witness in the world.*

But what does God expect of us? I think we get clued in on God's expectations in two places: Matthew 25 and 26.

In Matthew 25, Jesus told several parables just before he went to the Garden of Gethsemane and was arrested. The parables were told in this order: the parable of the ten virgins, the parable of the talents, and the parable of the sheep and the goats. Altogether, they were Jesus's final attempt to explain how his followers should live after he was no longer with them. I like to think of these as Jesus's *Remember who you are and whose you are* speech that so many parents give their kids before those kids go out in the world to do something big or scary. This speech involves three important points:

- **Stay alert.** The parable of the ten virgins is Jesus's way of highlighting that God expects us to prepare whatever is necessary to stay alert and present as we wait.
- **Contribute and participate.** The parable of the talents emphasizes that God expects us to use our talents to create an increase of his kingdom on Earth.

- **Remember what is at stake.** The parable of the sheep and the goats explains that our eternal connection to God is simultaneously revealed and determined by how we treat "the least of these" (Matt. 25:40 CSB).

Immediately after this speech, Jesus told the disciples, "You know that the Passover takes place after two days, and the Son of Man will be handed over to be crucified" (Matt. 26:2 CSB). He let them in on the spoiler that he was about to leave them and that they should get their lamps ready. He wanted them to dig up any talents they may have buried and be ready to make something more of them. He clued them in on the idea that not everyone who seems to know God does know God and that some of the people they trusted and respected may not treat Jesus the way he deserved to be treated.

But the disciples understood none of this. A woman anointed Jesus for his burial after the big speech of the parables, but death was not what any of them expected. So the disciples just kept on trucking. Shipshape. All systems go. They went to celebrate the Passover together. At the Passover table, Jesus attempted to let the disciples in on the spoiler that he was the Passover lamb, but they didn't get it. He pointed out Judas as his betrayer, but they couldn't think of a reason to doubt Judas's loyalty.

Jesus took them to the Garden of Gethsemane, where he prayed until he was troubled to the point of death. Jesus knew he was about to take on the greatest pain ever suffered. Any woman who has lain in a bathtub staring at her giant belly and considered the tiny exit path for the nine pounds of human being inside her has a small idea of what Jesus reckoned with as he prayed.

Birthing a world full of people will hurt more than I can imagine, Jesus must have thought.

Because it is not good for humans to be alone, Jesus asked Peter, James, and John to stay awake and pray for him in the garden. Jesus needed them to understand that they were living out the parables from Jesus's big speech. They were the virgins asked to keep watch. They were the servants entrusted with the responsibility of tending God's mission in the world. They were God's representatives, and how they cared for Jesus mattered to God because Jesus *was* God. But right there, during unprecedented events, incredible miracles, and the clearest explanations about the spiritual life, Peter, James, and John did not understand anything about Jesus's expectations of them or about what was happening.

They were tired, so they slept.

Thankfully, God has always written second chances into our lives. We see the second chance miracle in the lives of Peter, James, and John. They all deserted Jesus after they woke up and he was arrested. Peter denied he ever knew Jesus during the trial. But eventually, after his resurrection, Jesus appeared to them several times and explained everything to them. I do wonder how many times the disciples' heads spun with all they missed during their time following Jesus. I also wonder what we're missing about God's missional plans for the world right now.

Dear God, please help us to wake up to what you're doing around us. If we have slept through the important part, we ask for a second chance.

Driving Mercies

I scheduled an appointment for one of my teenage sons to get his driver's permit a few months ago. I signed him up for an online driver's education class and tasked him with finishing the requirements before the date of his appointment. On the eve of the appointment, he sheepishly mentioned that he was *almost* done with all the videos and assignments.

In response, I said, straight face intact, that government agencies don't generally give driving permits to people who have *almost* finished the requirements. I was a tiny bit irritated but did my best to be patient, kind, and clear about what needed to happen. He went to his room, finished the lessons, took the test, and told me all was good. Except it wasn't all good, because when we tried to print out the necessary documents for the appointment, he couldn't find them or figure out how to print them. My patience unraveled, and I fell asleep to God's call to mother with intentionality and patience. I forgot that God expected me to use my talents to increase the abundance of God's kingdom in my environment. I snoozed and released the truth that how I treat my son is how I have treated God.

In the world of parenting and motherhood, I believe tweaking that famous quote, "Heaven has no rage like love to hatred turned, nor hell a fury like a woman scorned,"[9] by William Congreve aptly describes my predicament that night. Had driver's licenses existed in his day, old Will would have said that hell hath no fury like a mother forced to reschedule with the DMV.

Somehow, my son and I trudged through the red tape, the emails, and the computer woes to get all the necessary documents. But we were not better for it. I felt worse than I had in months.

The morning of the appointment, I awoke and opened my Bible, expecting a sweet morning moment with the God who loves me so much. As I read the words of the Gospel of Matthew, I felt compelled to repent to God for my lack of kindness toward his son, who happens to also be my son. He is a teenager who is learning how to be an adult. He is one of God's favorite people, and he is worthy of kindness and patience. He's working so hard to learn how to be a quasi-adult, and I hadn't made space for him to fumble

---

[9] William Congreve, *The Mourning Bride* (London: Printed for Jacob Tonson, 1697).

the task at hand a little. When my son woke up, I apologized to him. I told him I wanted to be a gentler mother, even when the stress level rises. It was a gritty, spiritually rich moment for me.

My son had no idea what I was talking about. He thought everything was fine the night before. He graciously accepted my apology with a shrug of his shoulders and an "If it means that much to you, I forgive you, Mom."[10]

We arrived at our driver's permit appointment ten minutes early and took our number from the check-in desk. We sat in the only two open seats in the room. A rumor whispered its way around the room that the office had overbooked that day to meet quotas of some kind. After we waited for thirty minutes, my friend Leah walked in with one of her homeless friends. You may recall from Chapter Seven that Leah loves and serves the homeless community in Austin with incredible energy and excellence.

On that particular Friday, Leah brought her homeless friend Larry to the DMV for an ID card. Leah promised Larry it would only take ten minutes because on Fridays the lines are notoriously short. Leah and I sat across the room from one another, waiting for far too long. I sat with my son who forgave me despite my ridiculousness; she sat with a man in need of a mothering hand to guide him through the process of proving he is himself.

As I clutched documents that proved my guardianship of my son, his citizenship, his high school enrollment, and our address, that paperwork felt pithy in comparison with the boy beside me. The documents don't give the details, but I birthed this son of mine after a stormy night when my husband accidentally locked me out of our minivan in a face-melting storm. The contractions began after I was baptized in chaotic, literally horizontal rain. I birthed him through pain, and I have birthed him again and again through

---

[10] Sometimes God likes to call our bluff when we pray for him to humble us, and sometimes he likes to prank us a little.

sleepless nights, last-minute school projects, and now, DMV documents. As a mother, my job is to show up for my kids until the day my children know how to show up for themselves. And even then, I'll still be there.

Leah jokingly calls herself a homeless concierge, but in my mind, she simply shows up for the homeless of our city the way a mother should show up for her children. Leah takes them to the doctor. She is the person they call when they get in trouble with the police. Leah helps them fill out paperwork to obtain necessary documents such as identity cards, birth certificates, and veterans' benefits. Leah manages all their mail, lugging it around in her car to pass out later. When stimulus checks were sent out in 2020, Leah was the most popular woman in Austin when she arrived at the camps with checks in hand.

Showing up is what Jesus did for humanity when he, the Lord of heaven and Earth, chose to become a man and show up as a sacrifice capable of taking away our sins. It's what the church does for its community when it shows up to pay the rent of the unemployed, provide mentoring for struggling kids, and speak out against injustice.

The tangled and complex truth is that any time we show up with good intentions and a compassionate heart to meet a need in another person's life, we receive something that benefits us. Where else but in missional work can we find deeper gratitude, a broader perspective, or the uncanny hope that showing up for others proves to ourselves that we, too, are worth showing up for? Where else but in sacrificial love do we taste the belonging that holds all the longings of the human heart to never be left alone? How else but by helping one person at a time can we make the pain of the big, intimidating world seem a little smaller and easier to manage?

God's call to live out his mission in the world does not mean we must fix all the problems in the world. It just asks us to stay awake and be obedient to Jesus. But let's really tackle the lingering doubt we battle when we fight to stay awake and live out God's mission, which is this: How can we find the appropriate rhythm for missional giving and loving while also living our normal, every-day lives?

Fat Cats and Other Tales of Failure

In 1997, I was a twenty-one-year-old college student with a knack for navel gazing. Life challenged me back then, and I had many feelings about it. I navigated impossible college classes like Spanish Literature of the Golden Age (which was taught 100 percent in Spanish). I worked as a nanny every day after class, but I never made enough money to live in Los Angeles. I had a wicked awful plumbing bill because one of my roommates flushed a tube of deodorant down the toilet of the bathroom she never cleaned. I faced the daily burden of parallel parking my 1989 Acura Integra in my neighborhood next to the UCLA campus. I alone carried the responsibilities of adulting back then: grocery shopping, paying my bills, and deciding what to do with my hair. It was a stressful time.

If you're thinking my life back then sounds like normal adult life, not tragic at all, you would be correct. However, my hobby has always been summoning tragedy and drama from the quotidian. Jesus turned water into wine, and I turned normal life into a CW drama. It's my superpower, really.

One afternoon, I took a walk with my mentor, Suzanne, and I confided in her about the unfairness of life. Suzanne asked for specifics, and I explained about the dishes my roommates ignored, my job that didn't pay enough, my Spanish literature professor who insisted on teaching only in Spanish, and my trials involving parallel parking.

"You're a fat cat, spiritually speaking," Suzanne said. "You feel sorry for yourself because your whole life is about you. If you found ways to offer people some of the goodness inside you, you would feel so much better."

Wise Suzanne had been right, but after that fateful walk, I struggled to learn how not to live my life as a story all about me, my needs, and my feelings. Looking back, it amazes me how my twenty-one-year-old self felt no compulsion to do much of anything for others. I was stuck a little in my own immaturity for a few years.[11] I made baby steps toward helping and caring for others after I graduated, but when I married a man who worked as a full-time college campus minister, God blew me out of the waters of self-involvement for good. Ironically, by the time I was thirty, I found myself mentoring self-involved college students who were plagued by demanding professors, insufficient financial resources, bothersome roommate woes, and tragic hair stories.

God has a great sense of humor, no?

While doing too little to serve others was my struggle in my twenties, it isn't the only way we can lose our place in God's dance of mission in the world. It can be tempting to use missional service to try to save ourselves. I have known countless people who have used "serving God and others" as an excuse to neglect their souls, their physical health, the well-being of their friends and families, and the practical needs of life in general. When self-inflicted suffering is the result of overworking in ministry or over-volunteering in some area of ministry, our lives are not pleasing to God. This circumstance is evidence of a hidden, dysfunctional deception

---

[11] If you have an immature person in your life, I hope my story helps you have patience for their maturity to catch up with their heart for God. But also, I hope you'll be the kind of friend to them that Suzanne was to me.

about God's missional heart for the world—namely, that people are expendable to him and only useful so long as they're doing something to build his kingdom. When near-burnout becomes a badge of honor in our churches and ministries, we have made an idol of our productivity.

At other times, we lose the rhythm of God's mission by forgetting the goal of missional work entirely. Being the hands and feet of Jesus is supposed to be about showing God's love, not proving we're right about everything. This brings me to social media and complicated things that happen there regarding mission, evangelism, and theology.

I'm not sure exactly when social media platforms became the place we go to tell everyone how to do everything the right way, but that's where we've ended up. We mean well when we post articles about issues we're passionate about in an attempt to raise awareness. We mean well when we confront what we believe to be fake news or incorrect conclusions about an important topic of religious, moral, or cultural debate. We mean well when we try to use our platform to right what we see is wrong in the world. But surely, by now, we can see that our good intentions rarely communicate God's heart toward the people who disagree with us.

Like the proverbial church members who became enemies after debating the decision to recarpet the sanctuary, we are the most lost to one another when we are certain we are the most right before God. But if God is first and foremost a community of three dancing in our midst, willing us to join him in his dance of loving unity, our disconnection from one another is much more dangerous than we may realize. When we let go of the importance of belonging together, we are no longer following God's lead.

When our rhythm gets thrown off and we lose our place in the dance, how can we reconnect with God and others to engage in God's mission?

Golden Calves

To answer this question, let's flip back in our Bibles to Exodus 32–34, when all sorts of crazy stuff happened after the Israelites lost their place in God's dance.

Our story begins when Moses went up on a mountain to meet with God. God's finger inscribed his laws on two stone tablets, and Moses carried ten laws back home as party favors. However, while he was with God, the Israelites pressured Aaron into making an idol for them. Aaron lived by the "give the people what they want" code of leadership. He ground up all their jewelry, threw it into the fire, and created a golden calf. The Israelites then worshiped the calf as the source of their deliverance.

A lot of horrible events occurred after this. Moses shattered the tablets in anger. Three thousand rebellious men were killed for their treasonous acts against God. God was fairly ticked off, honestly.

Apparently, God figured the golden calf was evidence that the Israelites needed an object or a place associated with their faith that they could see and touch. Or maybe he wanted a place to talk to Moses closer to the camp because Uncle Aaron couldn't be trusted to babysit any longer. Whatever the reason, in Exodus 33:7–11, God had Moses pitch a tent outside the camp and call it the tent of meeting.

Just as moving into a new house makes us feel like we can make a fresh start, God and Moses began again in the tent of meeting. God gave Moses a little pep talk in there. He told him to cut new stone tablets and meet him on Mount Sinai the next day. In Exodus 34:6, God arrived in a cloud and called himself the Lord. Then he reintroduced himself to Moses the way someone in an awkward group therapy session would. What I'm trying to say is that the Lord went straight to the nitty-gritty, possibly overshared a little to achieve clarity, and even talked about himself in the third person:

> The LORD—the LORD is a compassionate and gra-
> cious God, slow to anger and abounding in faithful
> love and truth, maintaining faithful love to a thousand
> generations, forgiving iniquity, rebellion, and sin. But
> he will not leave the guilty unpunished, bringing the
> consequences of the fathers' iniquity on the children
> and grandchildren to the third and fourth generation.
> (Exod. 34:6–7 CSB)

What is the first word God used to define and describe himself just after his favorite people kicked him to the curb in favor of a shiny cow? He said he was "compassionate." The Hebrew word for compassionate in Exodus 34:6 is *rahum*. It's an adjective often used to describe God and is only ever translated as "compassion-ate." What makes this word interesting is that its root is the word *rehem*, which means "womb."

When God reintroduced himself to Moses, after the people lost their minds in rebellion, he described himself as womblike. God promised struggling people that he was a safe place for them to be nurtured and reborn. The Israelites had lost their way in the dance. They forgot that God sent plagues to deliver them. They forgot the Lord caused death to pass over their homes. They forgot the way the Red Sea split in two so they could escape to safety. God had led them in a beautiful waltz, but they went two-stepping with a cow.[12]

Exodus 32–34 is a good reminder that any time God's people struggle, the foolishness and sin we fling into the world are not wild bulls in God's first rodeo. God is always ready to welcome us

---

[12] I throw no shade on two-stepping. I love it so much. #90scountryforever

back from the golden calves we may have created in the fires of our lives because he is like a womb, and birthing new life is what wombs do.

Daring to be a person who passes out those spiritual tacos God's been stacking up inside of us is painful because I would rather be comfortable and make myself happy most days. Working to balance personal growth and missional efforts is hard work, and it often makes my head hurt. Choosing to build bridges instead of making a point on social media hurts like crazy. But then I remember: the pain is where God wants us to push. And mission takes some pushing. Or maybe a lot.

But the good news is that once we commit to that process, the birthing is up to God, not us. Our daddy momma God's womblike compassion will see it through. That's when things get fun and maybe a little messy, like my college roommates.

Now, it's time for some real talk about the messiness of mission.

CHAPTER

Tacos
of Endurance

Buddy: "I like smiling. Smiling's my favorite."

Gimbel's manager: "Make work your favorite. That's your favorite, okay? Work is your new favorite."

—*Elf*[1]

I have personally been involved in countless missional efforts in the twenty-seven years I have followed Christ. Some were miraculously successful and encouraging. Others fell a little flat. Missional work is a great place to learn that good intentions and honest effort don't consistently pan out as well as we would like.

For example, as a college student, I was a part of an evangelistic outreach in which we advertised a Christian speaker who was a former *Playboy* centerfold. Please try to imagine our shock and surprise when the visitors who showed up that night were mostly seeking a voyeuristic laugh and were not at all curious about the woman's faith. We were naive, but we meant well.

---

[1] *Elf*, directed by Jon Favreau (2003; Burbank, CA: New Line Cinema).

My early years as a Christian during the strange era of the 1990s involved kissing dating goodbye to allow God's missional heart to bring me a husband at just the right time. This method of finding love worked out for me, but I have a list of friends who didn't fare as well as I did. Purity culture tangled them up and wounded them quite a bit. We were hopeful but shortsighted.

Somewhere in the middle of my thirties, I bought a T-shirt with the text "147 Million" printed on it because there were (supposedly) 147 million orphans in the world. Part of the proceeds from that shirt's purchase raised money to help people adopt internationally. A few years later, the topic of Western Christians pursuing international adoption became sticky and messy. Shirts were no longer a clear way to reach out and help. We were confused but still wanted to help.

Some missional movements and efforts endure, while others fall apart for a variety of reasons. But even the ones that last must change or shift their approach every few years when old methods are found to be unhelpful or unhealthy.

Over the years, I have been disappointed that our missional efforts rarely effect the kinds of big change we dream of achieving in the world.

At some point between 1994 and 2021, I realized my perspective on missional work needed to shift. I began to ask God how we ought to pursue missional lives with hopeful, expectant faith as we hold the reality that we may not see the big impact we long to see God accomplish. In a way, Jesus once answered this question when two men declared their intention to follow him:

As they were traveling on the road someone said to him, "I will follow you wherever you go."

Jesus told him, "Foxes have dens, and birds of the sky have nests, but the Son of Man has no place to lay his head." Then he said to another, "Follow me."

"Lord," he said, "first let me go bury my father."

But he told him, "Let the dead bury their own dead, but you go and spread the news of the kingdom of God."

Another said, "I will follow you, Lord, but first let me go and say goodbye to those at my house."

But Jesus said to him, "No one who puts his hand to the plow and looks back is fit for the kingdom of God." (Luke 9:57–62 CSB)

First of all, props to Jesus for validating his everyday reality with that first guy. I'm grateful we have a savior who told people, *You want to follow me? I have no place to rest, buddy! This is not a play-date we're engaging in.* At the same time, this story fills my heart with empathy for our fully God/fully human Lord. I wonder if he wished for a place to lay his human head and rest from the weight of his future. I also wonder if, as he watched the comings and goings of people from the beginning of creation, Jesus had already seen that, in this world, we cannot attain the kind of rest our souls long for most of all.

The trouble with people is that we make messes everywhere, even when we have good intentions. If it wasn't Cain envying Abel's sacrifice so much that he killed him, it was Leah and Rachel playing "Babyopoly," trying to see who could pass go with the most sons first and win bragging rights. If it wasn't Peninnah pestering Hannah about her childlessness, it was David killing Uriah because he didn't want to get caught as a cheater.

In the spirit of this Luke 9 passage, let us recall that Jesus did not live an easy life full of comfort and devoid of struggle. Israel had been conquered by Rome, and the Jewish people were oppressed by Caesar. When Jesus was a baby, Herod, intent on killing Jesus, murdered all baby boys. When cultural oppression and political targeting weren't directly aimed at him, his fellow Jews threatened to stone him for preaching strange things about God being his Father. His popularity was fragile and spotty through the years of his public ministry. One day, the crowds were in awe of him, laying palm branches before him, and the next day, they were bloodthirsty, demanding his crucifixion.

Our desires to fix broken systems, save lost people from their brokenness, feed the hungry, liberate the captives, find homes for the homeless, place orphans in families, and contribute in a meaningful way are noble and good, as was the man's desire to follow Jesus in Luke 9. But Jesus told that man, in essence, that the real trouble we face is that the Messiah and his followers have nowhere to rest their heads.

Just in case we missed what Jesus was saying, Luke immediately tells us about another man who wanted to follow Jesus but felt obligated to bury his father first. Jesus was pretty clear when he suggested the man let the dead bury their own dead and instead spread the news of the kingdom of God. There are days when I wonder if Jesus was too hard on that man, telling him a person intent on looking back isn't fit for God's kingdom. But then I think of all the needs in the world, and I realize Jesus is casting a particular kind of vision: our missional loyalty to God is measured in our commitment to press forward in faith despite the failures of the past.

Jesus's words in Luke 9 linger long with me. Each time I read them, I am compelled to ask myself, my friends, and my family this: How can our lives be places where Christ and other people can rest their heads so they have strength for what lies ahead?

As I write this chapter, my husband is leading a church through the challenging era of COVID-19. We have all learned and grown so much along the way. Our daily lives disconnected themselves from other people for many months. The ways we arrive at church and community have shifted. In March 2020, we had to shift from all our meetings and events occurring in person to online-only overnight. When we first returned to real live people in the church on Sunday mornings, social distancing was in full effect. We required reservations, screened for COVID-like symptoms, took temperatures at the door, and required masks. We now have a hybrid of in-person and online Sunday services and events. We encourage but do not require masks. The room is full, although the additional cameras and equipment for our livestream limit the seating a bit now. We agonize regularly over how to shepherd and pastor a community of people with diverse opinions and ideas about what kinds of decisions keep us most safe while also honoring one another's diverse needs and viewpoints.

Some precious, beloved friends have left our church community because they want a church with a different approach to the pandemic. Others have left because, after meeting online for so long, their hearts lost their connection to our community. They don't feel a need for our community any longer. There are nights I lie awake and wonder if they understand that I, personally, still feel a deep need for them.

We have recently begun to have in-person events and classes outside of Sunday mornings again. Community groups are meeting face-to-face again. We've had parties in our parking lot, men's and women's events, and nights of worship. In some ways, these gatherings feel familiar, but there is an asterisk on the end of everything we do because nothing is the same as it was before illness changed the world.

Our efforts to reach our community and accomplish God's mission to love and serve our city have continued throughout the last eighteen months. Our staff and volunteers have cared for the neediest people in our city, cared for our local schools, organized a town hall with local police chiefs and racial justice activists to help us all find a way through together, and raised tens of thousands of dollars to combat poverty in our city. Our church has provided on-site licensed therapists for those who've needed counseling, paid bills for people left out of work, visited the sick, prayed for the hurting, and continued to support and fund missionaries in the United States and abroad.

But there are many days that we feel discouraged about almost everything because it's impossible to forget that no matter what we do, there is always more we could do for someone, somewhere. Following Jesus means living with the sound of a loud, banging drum just outside your window. Every beat declares there are more needs, more conflicts, more losses, and more pain. This spiritual race is long, and the path is arduous.

Paul admitted that the sacrifice required in the spiritual race we run is exhausting. In 1 Corinthians 9, he listed all the ways he sacrificed and gave himself to preaching the gospel to people. Then he said, "Now I do all this because of the gospel, so that I may share in the blessings. Don't you know that the runners in a stadium all race, but only one receives the prize? Run in such a way to win the prize" (1 Cor. 9:23–24 CSB).

As a former track athlete, I appreciate the race metaphor. I like the idea of having a course set that I must complete. I love that there is a prize for running well.

What I don't love as much is that the stopwatch seems a little broken.

Hurdles and High Bars

My parents took me to my first track practice when I was eight years old. I started running the two-hundred-meter "dash" and the four-hundred-meter "run," but for the next thirteen years of my life, I ran almost every race there was at some point or another. Something about a stopwatch confirming I had succeeded or failed satisfied my soul. I knew myself best when the numbers on a little clock in my coach's hand declared I had nailed my interval times. Race times were equally delicious for my soul, which seemed to have one request: clock me and see if I can beat my old personal best. *I want to win.*

By the time I was in high school, I high-jumped and ran both hurdle races, the four-hundred-meter, the eight-hundred-meter, and the anchor leg on the mile relay.

This was the early 1990s in Southern California, and at many track meets, I watched in awe as future Olympian and total world beater Marion Jones crossed the finish line twenty meters in front of her competitors. She was a wondrous sight to behold. I did not possess the same talent, but watching her made me want to run more, not less.

When I was recruited as a heptathlete at the University of Houston, I jumped (pun intended, sorry) at the opportunity to find out if I could make the time on the clock match the hope in my heart that running a race could prove my worth.

As it turned out, I wasn't good enough at those events to win. I struggled as an athlete in college. But during my time in Houston, I heard the gospel for the first time from a teammate. I began to believe that I didn't need a stopwatch to tell me I had value. Mine is the story, really, of how God uses our desire to be known and valued to lead us to all the ways earthly crowns will dissolve and fail us. When I chose to go to Houston, I could not comprehend the pain of failure I would experience there as an athlete. Losing and failing on the track felt like losing and failing myself. God asked me to forget the numbers when he invited me to join a new kind of race.

Many of us still try to run our spiritual race to get the best times. We do more and more good deeds to try to get ahead and prove we're good enough to be on the team. This is not the way of Christ's mission. It is a race but of a different kind with a different "clock."

Stop the Clock

Now that my athletic "career" is over, my sons' lives are the place where clocks and stopwatches come into play, and not always for the best. The clock involved in any sport (and you know this if you have ever sat through a high school basketball game) is a frustrating thing. Four minutes and twenty-five seconds of game time could take half an hour to play. The clock will stop when an incomplete pass is thrown in football. It will stop when the other team purposely fouls in basketball. At the little league baseball level, the clock is a mysterious thing in the umpire's pocket, and frankly, I have suspected many umpires disregarded the actual numbers and invented more time in an inning over the years.[2] Go ahead, call me a crazy sports mom. I can take it.

But here we are, two thousand years into the second half of God's playbook on Earth, and some days it seems like the final whistle will never blow.

Yesterday I woke up with a knot between my shoulders caused by several extra sets of pushups the day before. The physical knot only compounded my knotted-up soul. With an overloaded schedule of ministry duties, parenting responsibilities, and writing tasks, I buckled under the weight of a brutal and unrelenting clock. I spoke aloud to no one in particular: "I don't want to do this. All I want to do is lie in bed."[3]

---

[2] While I have yapped respectfully at many umpires over the years, I have only ever won one argument with an ump. There is nothing more satisfying than an ump apologizing profusely for his horrible calls. I cherish the memory still. #greatestmomever

[3] Can I trademark this phrase and put it on a T-shirt? Or maybe this could be the title of my next book!

I lay down on the floor of my bedroom to stretch my shoulders. Spontaneous tears welled up in my eyes. A sob formed in my throat. I was depleted of energy to care for myself and others. I was starving while surrounded by a hungry crowd, but the bag of spiritual tacos in my hand contained only empty wrappers. Can you relate to this kind of soul exhaustion? How can we make it to the end? When will the race be finished? When will the whistle blow? We simply have no idea. There is more time on the clock than we can guess. Maybe the reason God has hidden the clock from us is that counting down the seconds will not make a victorious finish to our spiritual race any easier to achieve.

But something else can.

Let's return to the passage we began with way back in the first chapter of this book.

> Very truly I tell you, you will weep and mourn while
> the world rejoices. You will grieve, but your grief will
> turn to joy. A woman giving birth to a child has pain
> because her time has come; but when her baby is born
> she forgets the anguish because of her joy that a child
> is born into the world. So with you: Now is your time
> of grief, but I will see you again and you will rejoice,
> and no one will take away your joy. In that day you
> will no longer ask me anything. Very truly I tell you,
> my Father will give you whatever you ask in my name.
> (John 16:20–23 NIV)

Remember when we talked about God's mission being like childbirth? Birthing women know grief and suffering that turns to joy after seemingly endless contractions. They understand the frustration of not knowing when the whistle will blow because they cannot see where the baby is in the birth canal. But this verse also reminds me of all my friends who have battled infertility and longed for a day they are not sure will ever come. Mission is sometimes like birthing new life, and other times, mission is like a hidden longing for a child while we have no idea how the story will get us there.

I recall a friend who wrapped up her broken heart in intangible soul Bubble Wrap as she went to a baby shower for yet another pregnant friend. How well she understood what Jesus spoke about in John 16 when he said the disciples would weep and mourn while the world rejoiced. Her courage to hurdle over her fear and doubt so she could show up for a friend birthed life into the world that most of us won't understand on this side of eternity. My friend had learned to stop keeping score. She laid down her biological clock. She refused to run the race like her value was measured by how quickly and efficiently her womb produced the miracle of life. She hid herself in God, and she trusted her story was held within his own. She is a hero in every possible way.

In many ways, we run our race alone with only the lifeline of the gospel to sustain us until Christ returns to show us the clock. I want us to end our race with our legs depleted and wobbly, our arms upraised, gasping for air, and shouting with victory. Lung capacity is the key to this achievement and is affected by what we believe about the end of this world's story.

In Revelation 12, we read a man named John's vision of what he called a great sign in heaven. The scene painted involves a woman clothed with the Sun and crowned with stars, groaning with the pain of childbirth. A fiery dragon crouched in front of the woman, ready to consume her child. She birthed a son, and God took him up to his throne. The woman fled to the wilderness, and war broke out between the angels of team archangel Michael and those of team dragon. John told us that the dragon lost and was thrown down to the Earth along with all his angels. Then John revealed that the dragon's true identity was Satan. After Satan's defeat, John heard a loud voice say this:

> The salvation and the power and the kingdom of our God and the authority of his Christ have now come, because the accuser of our brothers and sisters, who accuses them before our God day and night, has been thrown down. They conquered him by the blood of the Lamb and by the word of their testimony; for they did not love their lives to the point of death. Therefore rejoice, you heavens, and you who dwell in them! Woe to the earth and the sea, because the devil has come down to you with great fury, because he knows his time is short. (Rev. 12:10–12 CSB)

The dragon in Revelation didn't breathe fire like the ones in fairy tales. This dragon attacked the woman with water. He tried to wash her away in a flood. The Earth itself opened up to swallow the water so she could escape. The Bible then says, "So the dragon was furious with the woman and went off to wage war against the rest of her offspring—those who keep the commands of God and hold firmly to the testimony about Jesus" (Rev. 12:17 CSB).

What does this wild heavenly vision mean for us and our desire to fulfill God's call to love and serve the world missionally?

Those of us who keep God's commands and believe Jesus is the Christ dance with the triune God and all his angels on the front lines of a spiritual warzone. No wonder our souls are gnawed at by intimidation and weariness. We face a powerful enemy who wants nothing more than to sweep us away in a flood.

To prevail in this fight, it's important to remember that we serve a more powerful God who already won the final battle. It's also vital to recall that every time we reach our hands out to love and care for another person, we remind the dragon that he was thrown down in defeat long ago.

We hear it quoted often, but we don't always consider what Revelation is pointing at when it says God's people "conquered [Satan] by the blood of the lamb and by the word of their testimony; for they did not love their lives to the point of death." This voice from heaven is hinting at the importance of mission in the spiritual realm.

We conquer Satan using a threefold attack. To truly live missional lives, we need the blood of Jesus, the truth about our stories, and to live like eternity matters more than our current earthly lives.

Bloody Love

I took Communion surrounded by my church family yesterday. Forgive the existential crisis, but my inner emptiness sideswiped my thoughts like an eighteen-wheeler on ice. I peeled back the purple foil on the tiny cup of grape juice, and that tablespoon-sized serving of Communion juice seemed inadequate to fill all the space within me that longed for divine intervention. In a moment of graphic honesty, I asked God to fill me with his bloody sacrifice as I stood frozen in my new winter boots.

Have I gone too far with this gory faith imagery? Along with Jesus chatting about drinking his blood and eating his flesh, our faith is full of graphic and strange blood metaphors, so I feel I'm in good company. Consider Colossians 2:11, which teaches that spiritual circumcision makes us whole in Christ. If you've never witnessed the screams of a baby being circumcised, you may be lulled into a false sense of sweetness that Paul never intended when he penned that image. And if we look in the Bible for how to get close to God, Ephesians 2:13 makes it clear that no one rides without a Messiah blood train ticket.

Arguably, the most horrific part of the gospel is how bloody personal it is. We can't separate our faith from suffering and the spilling of blood. We ought to expect our spiritual journeys to involve suffering. However, in our modern world, where the sight of blood and pain is generally hidden inside hospitals, we are unaccustomed to its presence in our daily lives. We often want to believe our faith can be as clean and comforting as fresh sheets on an organic mattress. We want to offer the world good news about how loved and special they are to God. We do not want to be the people who tell others they are sinners. We don't want to invite them to be spiritually circumcised. We shy away from suggesting that their invitation to God's presence was written in blood on the body of an innocent man who was executed by the government.

But if we leave out the truth about the bloody sacrifice of Jesus, we send people into a spiritual war without the primary weapon capable of defeating the dragon attacking them. This is partly why Communion should be a powerful practice. We take some juice or wine and pour it down our throats, and the memory of the blood necessary for our salvation fills us and grants us access to the second weapon necessary to defeat the dragon.

When God Talks Trash

Your testimony is a holy weapon in the heavenly realm. I'm not talking about the story of your life, nor am I implying that you should write a memoir and sell it as a holy book. I mean that God regards your spiritual life as a holy witness of how his power and presence eradicated sin and selfishness from your eternal reality. We could even assume God uses your faithfulness as a fountain of trash talk against Satan. If you doubt our God brags about his kids being awesome, this passage from Job 1:6–12 (NIV) proves otherwise:

One day the angels came to present themselves before the LORD, and Satan also came with them. The LORD said to Satan, "Where have you come from?"

Satan answered the LORD, "From roaming throughout the earth, going back and forth on it."

Then the LORD said to Satan, "Have you considered my servant Job? There is no one on earth like him; he is blameless and upright, a man who fears God and shuns evil."

"Does Job fear God for nothing?" Satan replied. "Have you not put a hedge around him and his household and everything he has? You have blessed the work of his hands, so that his flocks and herds are spread throughout the land. But now stretch out your hand and strike everything he has, and he will surely curse you to your face."

The LORD said to Satan, "Very well, then, everything he has is in your power, but on the man himself do not lay a finger."

Every time I encounter this passage, I am struck again by how proud and confident God sounds when he talks up his son Job. He sounds like a basketball coach who believes his player will hit double digits even if faced with the best defender in the league. He sounds like the parent of a well-trained musician, sure that his child can produce world-class music from any instrument available. He is the friend who insists your chocolate cake is so good it could win a blue ribbon at the state fair even if you competed against the greatest pastry chefs in the nation. When God brags about us to that dragon named Satan, he holds up a people of holy submission to Christ.

When we read Revelation 12:11, we can consider the blood of Jesus and our testimony to be a double-edged sword because our testimony results from our allegiance to the centrality, authority, and supremacy of Christ's bloody sacrifice. Missional acts are the muscle we use to raise that sword against the floodwaters of evil in the world. With every thrust, we cut holes that drain the dragon water.

Now, because we have the blood of Jesus and the testimony of God's miraculous love, we prove we have all the weapons mentioned in Revelation 12:11 by valuing eternity above the temporary. After all, since Jesus is our home, this place where we live is just a pit stop.

Dancing in a Jalopy

My son and I were driving to church in Old Bessie recently, and as we accelerated to highway speed, the sunroof did the jackhammer thing I told you about.

"I hate this car!" my son shouted over the deafening sound of hammering above us.

I waited for the sound to stop, and then I told him he should love Old Bessie. "This car is the reason we can afford a car for you, your education, and all the other expensive things you love about your life. But yeah, that sound is the worst, isn't it?"

He was quiet for a moment. "Okay, I love this car," he conceded.

I smiled, thinking about the day we bought our old Toyota Sequoia. Our kids were so little back then. Life was simpler and yet more exhausting, with four kids under seven. Our old minivan had been totaled when a truck rear-ended us on the highway. We couldn't afford a car payment, so our budget for a new car was set at exactly the insurance payout total. I had visited a used car lot the week before, but they didn't have anything on the lot that worked for us in our price range. A few days later, someone traded in Old Bessie for a new Lexus. The salesman took one look at Bessie and thought of us immediately.

I had hoped Bessie would last five years when I drove her off the lot. She's still (loudly) cruising along ten years later. When I climbed into the driver's seat that day on the lot, I never could have imagined how much would change about my life, myself, and the world in ten years. I would have failed to imagine the awe Morgan and I would feel to have all our boys grow taller than both of us. I could not have processed the future pain of a pandemic. I would have laughed to hear how funny, smart, and kind my daughter would one day be. We lived in an unfixed-up fixer-upper back then. Had I seen photos of the big house we share with all these kids now, I might have swooned and reached for smelling salts like a character in a classic book. And if you had described how the love in my life would deepen even when the floodwaters rose to my nose and threatened to wash me away, I would not have believed you.

In the ten years I've driven this old beater of a car, I have learned to dance with God in this world that is nothing more than a cosmic jalopy. Just as my son understood that an old broken-down car was the key to receiving better blessings than a flashy new ride, I have mostly made my peace with the rattling and injustice of this life.

If this world were not so loud and painful, I would not dare to wrap my arms around God and try to follow his lead.

Today, my friend posted a photo on Instagram of his friend from India. The teen was wrapped in bandages after acid was used to burn him as a punishment for preaching the gospel in his town. His pain is incomprehensible. A few weeks ago, the United States border patrol rounded up Haitian refugees crossing the Mexican border on horseback. The images are heartrending. This week, a seventeen-year-old boy from my sons' high school committed suicide. The sorrow seems unbearable. I have prayed for the boy in India. I have raised money to care for refugees at the border. And my husband has reached out to the principal of the high school to see if there is any way our church can support the students and faculty as they mourn. None of these acts have cost me or my husband our lives. Entering the dance of God among these painful circumstances has only cost us some of our resources in the form of time, money, words, and emotional energy.

Just as I bought an old SUV because it was all we could afford and it has lasted us far longer than we expected, every missional act is the manifestation of the belief that we will all last far longer than most people here want to believe. We were made for eternity. Entering into the pain others experience in this life to ease their suffering sweetens the reunion we will share in the life to come.

I don't know what suffering you have borne witness to in your life. I wonder if people or causes are surfacing within your heart and mind as you read this book. If so, I hope and pray you will consider sowing your resources and join God's dance in whatever jalopy he leads you to. Somewhere, beneath the sunroof that rattles, inside the doors that don't always open, and with the people God put in that broken-down SUV with you, is God's mighty power over evil in your life and the world.

When we cross over into the future we have been promised with God, we will dance as the people God bragged about with a loud voice from heaven. It will sound something like this: *These are the ones who overcame evil by the blood of the lamb, the word of their testimonies, and their determination to live like God's kingdom had already come. Well done, good and faithful servant. Now join God's joyful and eternal dance.*

When Jesus, Love, & Tacos Dance

"Wake me up before you go-go
'Cause I'm not planning on going solo
Wake me up before you go-go
Take me dancing tonight."

—Wham![1]

In the summer of 2011, my husband's prayers were answered, and I danced in the rain with God and my kids.

I had spent the previous weeks explaining water to my children, teaching them the lesson from my own elementary school days, when I learned that water never goes away. I told my children about a coloring sheet Mrs. Heller passed out thirty years before with outlines of clouds raining down on a mountain. The rain became a stream as it ran down the mountain into a lake. Some of it seeped through the Earth into the water table. On the opposite

---

[1] "Wake Me Up Before You Go-Go," Wham, track 1 on Wham, *Make It Big*, Columbia, 1984.

side of the paper, the lake water evaporated back up into big, fluffy clouds. Just in case we needed the cycle to be made completely obvious, arrows pointed out which way the water headed in each part of the cycle. Water made an endless cycle in the world.

"The water dances through the world," I explained. "It gets recycled again and again."

We were in the middle of a drought in the summer of 2011. My young children needed to understand the importance of conservation so they wouldn't waste water or take it for granted. The temperature rose above one hundred degrees for sixty-nine consecutive days that summer. Climate experts blamed La Niña, but naming the cause did not change our circumstances. We were hot and desperate for rain.

Our family had just moved into a little 1970s ranch-style house surrounded by large live oak trees. Earlier in the year, I had marveled at how we seemed to live in the middle of a busy little ecosystem, with squirrels, birds, and bugs making noise all day long. But a heavy, hot silence descended on our mini forest that summer. There was no breeze to rustle the leaves or birds busily hunting worms in the early morning hours. At night, we didn't hear cicadas or crickets chirping. As the air got hotter and drier, the wildlife hid away, quietly waiting for a reprieve that did not come. The people followed suit, hunkering down inside where air-conditioned rooms kept us more comfortable than our ancestors would have been.

Local farmers desperately needed water, so the city drained our lakes to keep livestock and crops alive. Lake levels receded to all-time lows. The city asked residents to use less water to save our lakes. Water prices went up, up, up. Wildfires raged through ancient forests outside the city. Four million acres of Texas land blazed in 2011.

My husband heard through the church grapevine that the city had asked local pastors to come and pray for rain at a city council meeting. This rarely happens anywhere, let alone in Austin, Texas.

So, a group of pastors went to the meeting. They prayed for rain. Then they went home.

As unbelievable as this may be, the day after that meeting, fat raindrops fell on Austin. Lots and lots of them fell and kept falling. My kids and I ran into our front yard to dance in the downpour. We felt amazed and grateful.

The drought had revealed how powerless we were to control the water cycle. When divine rescue arrived, what could we do except join the dance?

Let's Make a Deal

The water cycle is a mirror of our spiritual lives. Just as water flows through the sky, the land, and all living creatures, God's love and being flow through our personal allegiance to Jesus, our devotion to building healthy communities, and our generous offering to love as we've been loved.

Water is always with us, doing things to make our world more livable, giving life to plants and creatures, filling lakes so we can water our crops and livestock, and giving us reasons to run outside to dance in gratitude. Likewise, God's great love rains down and flows into us from his triune eternal authority and power. That love does many things for all of us. It floods our lives and rushes down into our relationships to fill the reservoirs of our churches. As our churches navigate the waves of God's call to be a blessing to our cities, the filled-up, beloved people of God reach out their hands to love and serve the world, and God's love rises out of our lives as praise and glory to God. When this cycle is healthy and strong, the whole world benefits from its flow. When difficult seasons come, and when we can't see or sense God's love cycling through our lives, desperation and discouragement rise. But relief will always come eventually. As we wait, it's good to remember that we can't hurry God's replenishing love any more than we can hurry the rain.

Just as people can't exchange labor or money to coax a deluge of rain from the sky or flip a switch to turn off a hurricane, we can't pay God to love us more or less. Love, like water, cycles around us and through us as rivers we must navigate or as invisible vapors, which we breathe in and out with little notice.

We can't buy more love from God with more faith or better works.

> For while we were still helpless, at the right time, Christ
> died for the ungodly. For rarely will someone die for a
> just person—though for a good person perhaps some-
> one might even dare to die. But God proves his own
> love for us in that while we were still sinners, Christ
> died for us . (Rom. 5:6–8 csb)

God loves us while we're a mess. He loves us when we're asleep in the garden after he asked us to stay awake and pray. He loves us when we fail to love others as we love ourselves. He loves us when we're selfish and dumb and take everything too personally. He loves us when we're bossy. God loves us when we try to hide from him, and he loves us when we stomp and demand he do the thing we think he already should have done.

God flows all around us, whether we choose to dance in the waters or not. We can't buy rain, and we can't buy God. He is priceless in every possible way.

Can't Cut This Line, Honey

Just as people have gathered around lakes and ponds to do chores or enjoy a swim for centuries, God's priceless, loving, eternal authority facilitates and necessitates communal connection. What I mean is that God is a package deal. The flow of God in our individual lives creates pools we call a faith community, a church, or a spiritual family.

Our churches can't be bought or owned by the powerful or the wealthy. Unfortunately, many Christians who consider themselves mature see their tithes and offerings as a way to fund the kinds of sermons, programs, events, and ministries that meet their own life needs. They treat their local church like it's a vending machine and expect it to dole out just what they want and like. Other Christians look in the vending machine to make sure it's "the right kind of church," meaning it's a certain denomination, is a particular congregational size, elevates a specific cause as important to God, or espouses a particular political leaning. Also unfortunate is the way leaders with power and influence often imply that their churches belong to them, that their leadership might makes all their choices and decisions right. They try to own churches with their charisma and powerful talents. This creates dams and inhibits the flow of God's love into our churches and out from our churches.

You can't buy your belonging to the body of Christ with spare change or an easy smile. In a way, finding a church family is like following the river to the ocean and realizing how many of us can fit out on the expansive body of water before us. Church, like an ocean view, is a place to marvel at God's greatness, be refreshed and restored, and link arms with all the other people who are there to do the same thing.[2]

Mission Accomplished

When our churches are healthy, they function as places where the flow of God in people's personal lives overflows a community

[2]Both the beach and the church are places where some people think the music gets way too loud. #morecowbell

with God's being and heart. The natural result of this is God's missional outreach into a needy and thirsty world. Like the water that evaporates into the sky to make fluffy clouds, God's love fills our communities and rises to offer shade and fresh spiritual rain, and, ultimately, it rescues us from the blazing droughts created by life on this grueling planet.

Just like Jesus and church, we can't buy our way into or out of God's call to missional work. Christian hearts have been broken again and again when we've expected our missional work to either prove our worth or provide some prideful need for identity.

When missional work is taken up as a way to love the God who is love itself by caring for people in need of rescue and aid, the flow of God increases. The dance spirals upward, drawing our gaze to the clouds. Our spiritual minds fill with greater revelatory truth, and we see the way God is no respecter of persons. We launch spiritual tacos out into the hungry crowds. Our awareness that all people bear great worth to God makes us hungry to fulfill our one small part of the eternal celebration of his greatness.

In this way, mission fills the clouds with the rain of God's flow once more, and the cycle begins again. We fill and flow with God, and we are carried deeper into the divine community, which draws us deeper into the human community. This, in turn, opens our hands and hearts to loving and serving God's missional call in the world in new and fresh ways.

All the arrows on the spiritual water cycle point us from Jesus (aka submission to lordship) to love (aka community) and to tacos (aka missional acts). They are the stops on the cycle, or we could consider them the steps we've been asked to learn to join in the dance of God.

I Wanna Dance with Somebody

One cold winter night, when my children were still small, our family joined our church's street ministry team. We drove from stop to stop, serving people who lived in tents and under bridges, in cheap motels, or on someone's couch.

One man, "Sam," greeted Morgan with a great big bear hug. Sam and Morgan had met before and bonded over a shared love of baseball. On that particular night, Sam was grieving. He shared the story of how his friend died in the middle of the night, right beside him in a sleeping bag. He offered a cigarette to Morgan, even though he knew Morgan doesn't smoke. Sometimes a cigarette isn't just a cigarette; sometimes it's an invitation to dance.

I met a new homeless friend that night. "Sharelle" shared her story with me in bits and pieces. When she was twelve years old, her mom died and her dad kicked her and her sister out. "He's old school, you know," she said. "He said we should be able to make it on our own." Sharelle wasn't homeless any longer. She was married, had a baby, and lived in government housing. Sharelle bowed her head toward me conspiratorially as she shared that she and her husband rarely had food in the house. Then she laughed and held up the bag of groceries we had given her, like the challenges of poverty were also a delightful game of strategy.

My children filled cups with cocoa and handed out bags of clothing and food from the back of a pickup truck that night. The temperatures dropped as the hours ticked by. When it reached close to freezing, I herded them onto a patch of grass next to the gas station where a line of cold, hungry people had gathered. I wanted to get the kids moving to keep them as warm as I could.

"Let's do the hokey pokey!" I suggested.

That was how we ended up putting a left foot in and out and shaking it all about under a gas station sign on Research Boulevard while cars drove past and people waited for what they needed most. One wary couple slipped out of the nearby woods and joined our group. They stood holding their new food and blankets and watched us dance. I was purposely being silly to make my kids laugh because they had reached their limit for the night. We could barely feel our toes, but we were having fun. Morgan noticed the couple watching us and went to chat with them. The woman began to cry as she told him how secluded their lives were. "We stay in the woods most days, to avoid the way some people look at us. Can you believe it, that people are afraid of us? Thanks for bringing your kids tonight. It's good to remember what happy children look like."

I think about that couple a lot when I sit on my non-designer sofa and watch TikTok dances. I wonder if the same sense of connectedness and love they felt while watching my kids dance is what we long for as we scroll our way through our feeds with all those videos and reels with random strangers seemingly having the time of their lives, laughing and sharing truthful words meant to be both comforting and helpful. I wonder how many of the TikTokers we watch are trying to be extra silly to curb their own desperation and suffering as they offer the same relief to their followers.

Has our fear of what could happen piqued our longing for proof that there is a truth and a power that has already overcome the troubles we face? Has our shame and our lack of meaningful relational connection propelled us toward God's laughter and love dancing around us? Has our anger at the injustices we've witnessed or experienced driven us toward God's call to help and rescue the needy and the outcast?

Maybe TikTok hasn't ruined us after all. Maybe it's one of the millions of ways God is doing something for us, all day, every day, to alert us to his presence in the world. Our God is always at work, doing whatever he can to reach his hand out to invite us back into the eternal dance that is the I Am. It may be a stretch, but I hope that as we reach for our phones, for our Bibles, for our people, for our dinner, for our wallets, for our volunteer schedule, for our mission trips, and for ourselves, we will recognize our need to reconnect with our Lord, whose love has birthed us into his church and who has called us to live out his missional heart by offering the world the spiritual tacos it needs most of all.

This is the end of *Jesus, Love, & Tacos*. But, like all dances, like the water cycle, and like the promise of life after death, what seems like the end is also a chance to begin again, to reenter the flow and find ourselves filled and renewed.

Here's to dancing forever, together in Christ.

ACKNOWLEDGMENTS

When I first set out to write this book, I thought it would be an easy task. I'm pretty sure God laughed at me that day because he knew not a word of this book would come to me easily. In fact, I lost fifteen thousand words when my computer crashed repeatedly in the middle of 2021. I thought rewriting those chapters was the most impossible task I'd face until I died a thousand deaths editing my manuscript. The moral of the story is that there are no easy books to write, and also that God has high standards.

I offer my whole heart of gratitude to my husband for being the most wonderful editor in the world. It's always been you, Morgan. To my kids, who told me this book would be awesome before they ever read a word of it, thank you for having my back and insisting I have nothing to prove. I love you one bazillion.

To Mosaic Church, and specifically, the elders, staff, and volunteers, thank you for being my friends and family. You are the greatest miracle I've ever witnessed.

To my agent, Mary DeMuth, thank you for believing in me, rooting for me, and inviting me to be a part of your incredible team of authors. What a gift you've been to me! And to my publisher, Leafwood, thank you for the opportunity to write another book. Every writing opportunity is evidence of God's mercy and grace.

I lost two friends during the writing of this book, and their deaths will always be linked to this project in my heart. My friend Suzanne entered God's eternal presence like a true champion in 2021. She taught me about fat cats and orange skies as well as Coke floats and antique furniture. I miss her, and I hope the stories about her do her Christ-filled missional heart justice. My friend Keivon also finished his race in 2021. He was a wonderful writer, gifted pastor, great husband and dad, and all-around incredible person. Keivon was a beta reader for my first book, and I have missed his joy-filled feedback on this project.

To all the gorgeous, blessed people who read my books, thank you for reading! Your story is a holy thing, and I hope my words help you find God in new ways. Thank you for all the ways you've joined God's dance and let his love fill and overflow from your life. You're just wonderful, really.